Warren County, Tennessee

Marriages

1852 – 1865

Byron and Barbara Sistler

Byron Sistler & Associates, Inc.
1986

Warren County, Tennessee Marriages 1852-1865

Originally published, Nashville, Tennessee
1986

Reprinted by

Janaway Publishing, Inc.
732 Kelsey Ct.
Santa Maria, California 93454
(805) 925-1038
www.JanawayGenealogy.com

2006, 2011

ISBN: 978-1-59641-067-1

Made in the United States of America

WARREN COUNTY, TN MARRIAGES

1852-1865

Where two dates appear, the first one is the date license was issued, the second (in parentheses) the date marriage was solemnized. If only one date, it usually means that the date of execution was the same as the date of license issuance.

Sometimes the execution of the marriage was not reported to the court-house, and occasionally the clerk failed to note in the marriage book that the license was returned. We would usually make a notation in the entry to indicate the non-execution of a marriage if the book so stated.

The records included herein were transcribed by us directly from microfilm of the original marriage books. Error, where it occurs, may be attributed to us, or to the clerks of the period, many of whom did an appallingly sloppy job of entering the information.

If the bride and groom were black, a B is placed at the end of the entry.

It should be remembered that this and other marriage books we have prepared are essentially indexes and do not include all the information to be found in the original marriage book. Such data as names of bonds-men, ministers, justices of the peace, churches etc. is omitted. Often such information is helpful to the researcher. Consequently the serious researcher, to obtain this additional data as well as to check on the accuracy of the transcriber, should examine the original marriage record if at all possible, or at least another marriage record book which may contain this information.

Byron Sistler
Barbara Sistler

Nashville, TN
December, 1986

```
----- TO C. C. STARNES
----- TO JACKSON BARNES
-----, B. F. TO MISSIAN HICHCOCK 7-13-1858 (7-18-1858)
------, REDDING? TO ----- DODSON? 11-17-1862 (11-18-1862)
----GS, W. H. TO E. J. WARD 10-25-1859
-ANKHAM, LUCINDA TO EDWARD MCDANIEL
ADAMSON, JULIA A. TO J. R. CUNNINGHAM
ADCOCK, JULETT? TO JAMES M. ROBERTS
ADCOCK, MALETA TO FRANK MCDOWEL
ADCOCK, MALETTA TO FRANK MCDANIEL
ADCOCK, MARTHA ANN TO JOHN MARTIN
ADIER, JAMES TO MARTHA LOW 7-15-1854
ADISON, CYNTHIA TO WM. S. PEPPER
ADKINS, LUCINDA TO JERRY JACO
ADKINS, MARY TO FRANK MCDOWEL
ADKINS, MELVIN DALLAS TO MARY JANE JONES 12-4-1862
ADKINS, NANCY TO WILEY JACO
AIKINSON, KITTEY ANN TO ANDREW J. TURNER
AKEMAN, GEORGE W. TO MARTHA CARTRIGHT 6-6-1860 (6-7-1860)
AKEMAN, JOHN TO MARY JANE HIGGENBOTHAM 4-3-1856
AKEMAN, MARY TO JOHN L. HAYES
AKERS, A. A. TO J. C. MATHEWS
AKERS, ELIZABETH TO W. C. WEST
AKERS, MARY ANN TO R. W. HERNDON
AKERS, NANCY J. TO H. H. WILSON
AKERS, W. R. TO S. E. BARNES 3-19-1862
AKIN, JAMES TO ELIZA GUEST 7-24-1860
AKINSON?, GEORGE TO MARY GRAVES 1-7-1856 (1-8-1856)
ALEXANDER, ELIZABETH TO RICHARD M. BRAGG
ALEXANDER, EMILINE TO WILLIAM MCMAHAN
ALEXANDER, J. C. TO VIOLA H. WOOD 2-25-1863
ALEXANDER, J. M. TO E. A. MADUX 9-18-1860 (9-20-1860)
ALISON, M. C. TO WM. C. CLUCK
ALLEN, AMANDAH TO J. W. THOMASON
ALLEN, HESEKIAH TO NANCY J. SMITH 12-16-1862 (12-18-1862)
ALLEN, JAMES TO JANE ELLIS 9-6-1857
ALLEN, MARTHA JANE TO WASHINGTON BARNES
ALLEN, MARY TO ALEXANDER WALKER
ALLEN, WM. TO LOUIZA JANE MARTIN 6-1-1854
ALLEY, G. W. TO MARY BYBEE 7-15-1858
ALLISON, CLEMENTINE TO AARON A. PEPPER
ALLISON, KELLY TO ANNY KENNEDY 12-25-1858 (12-26-1858)
ALLISON, MARY TO M. M. SHERRELL
ALLISON, RACHEL TO JOHN WEBB
ALLS, SAMUEL TO NANCY MANNING 2-14-1860
AMONETT, TENNIE G. TO JAS. J. WOMACK
ANDERSON, ISAAC TO LAURA TATE 12-8-1854 (12-10-1854)
ANDERSON, ISAAC TO NANCY A. BRAGG 8-7-1856
ANDERSON, JAMES J. TO MARY J. JONES 7-29-1863
ANDERSON, LOUISA TO G. P. HOLMES
ANDERSON, POLLY TO JOHN BROWN
ANDERSON, SARAH O. TO ISHAM Y. CRAVEN
ANDERSON, W. B. TO NANCY E. HAMMER 12-6-1858
ARGO, ALICE M. TO E. G. BRENE?
ARGO, CORA F. TO SML. HENDERSON
ARGO, LAURA A. TO MONTGOMERY B. HARWELL
ARGO, LETTY TO WILIE WARE
ARGO, MARTHA TO ALBERT RAINS
```

Warren County, Tennessee, Marriages 1852-1865

ARMSTRONG, ANNA TO WILLIAM J. WOOD
ARMSTRONG, DRUCILLA TO JOHN GIBBS
ARMSTRONG, LAURA M. TO R. E. CAIN
BADGER, SOUSAN E. TO JEFFERSON JONES
BAGGARD, JOHN S. TO SARAH CHRISTIAN 9-14-1856
BAIN, JASPER TO MAXEY WILLIAMS 12-9-1856 (12-10-1856)
BALES?, JOSEPH TO AGNES C. STANDLY 5-19-1853
BALLOW, ALEXANDER TO GEMIMA JANE SMITH 4-4-1862 (4-6-1862)
BALLUE, D. C. TO MARY G. TATE 2-2-1859
BANES, MARY ANN TO WM. W. L. MARTIN
BANIS?, SARAH TO JOHN M. BOWERS
BANKS, FRANCES TO ALEXANDER BROWN
BANKS, FRANCES TO ALEXANDER? BROWN?
BANKS, M. C. TO MARGARET SEALS 11-5-1853 (11-6-1853)
BANKS, STEPHEN TO H. AMANDAH TROTT 8-2-1856
BARKER, FRANCIS M. TO MAHALA MILLER 3-15-1856
BARKER, JOHN TO REBECCA VANHOOSER 9-17-1861 (9-18-1861)
BARKSDALE, F. M. TO NANCY GIBSON 11-25-1858 (11-24?-1858)
BARNES, ISAAC TO SUSANNAH HILL 5-20-1853 (5-21-1853)
BARNES, JACKSON TO ----- 12-30-1855
BARNES, JACKSON TO CORA BESS 2-19-1856 (2-21-1856)
BARNES, JACKSON TO CORAH JANE BESS 1-1-1856
BARNES, LOUVISA TO A. J. WOODLEE
BARNES, MARTHA ANN TO ADAM MAYFIELD
BARNES, S. E. TO W. R. AKERS
BARNES, WASHINGTON TO MARTHA JANE ALLEN 3-18-1854
BARNES, WM. C. TO BETHIA HILL 2-4-1859 (2-5-1859)
BARNES, WM. C. TO ELIZABETH JACOBS 5-6-1862 (5-11-1862)
BARRETT, EMALINE TO JAMES LYNN
BARRETT, J. H. TO R. E. LANCE 10-6-1865 (10-7-1865)
BARRETT, JESSEE TO MARY E. WEST 2-24-1863
BARRETT, SARAH E. TO ARCHABLE F. CATHEY
BARROTT, JOHN TO MANERVA STOTTS 1-2-1855 (2-4-1855)
BASSHAM, JAMES? M. TO MISSABYLE STARKEY 9-13-1852 (9-14-1852)
BATES, ELIZABETH TO J. S. LANCE
BATES, L. F. TO J. R. RASCO
BEAM, MARTIN A. TO MARY D. BURLISON 8-13-1855
BEAM, MARY M. D. TO AARON BOLEN
BELL, JAMES M. TO ANN BONNER 12-1-1856 (12-4-1856)
BELL, JEREMIAH TO HANNAH NEAL 6-12-1857 (6-14-1857)
BELL, LOUIZA J. TO SEMERAL M. ROBERTS
BELL, LUCINDA TO W. D. ROBERTS
BELL, MARY TO THOS. HARRISON
BELL, SARAH TO RICHARD POTTER
BELL, T. J. TO SARAH E. THAXTON 7-26-1858 (8-3-1858)
BELL, WILLIAM H. TO SARAH SHRADER 1-3-1866
BELL, WILLIAM TO ELIZA TANNER 11-20-1858 (11-21-1858)
BELOTE, W. S. TO MARTHA F. SMITH 3-17-1860 (3-18-1860)
BENNETT, EMMA E. TO SAMUEL DAVIS?
BESS, CORA TO JACKSON BARNES
BESS, CORAH JANE TO JACKSON BARNES
BESS, LOUISA TO ARCHABALD MCGEE
BESS, LOUIZA TO TOMAS J. EDINGTON
BESS, NANCY TO ISAAC RHEA
BESS, THOMAS TO FRANCES MULLICAN 1-22-1859 (1-23-1859)
BESS, W. C. TO CAROLINE WEBB 5-19-1860 (5-20-1860)
BIFORD, MARGARETT TO S. B. MARCOMB
BIFORD, MARGARTT J. TO S. B. MARCOMB
BILES, E. B. TO ELSBERRY LAYNE
BILES, ELIZABETH TO HENRY BROWN

BILES, J. A. TO C. S. MATHEWS 7-19-1857
BILES, J. P. TO SARAH J. HUMBLE 9-15-1860 (9-16-1860)
BILES, JOSEPH TO JANE HENNESSEE 4-28-1856
BILES, SARAH A. TO P. M. MYERS
BINKLEY, FRANKLIN TO PARALEE SMITH 8-3-1863
BISHOP, EUPHEMEA ANN TO ARCHD. RHEA
BISHOP, JOHN E. TO VINEY STONER 1-15-1857
BISHOP, POLLY TO ISAAC BROWN
BISHOP, REBECCA TO CHARLES FOSTER
BISHOP, SARAAH TO J. J. TUITUR
BISHOP, SARAH TO ISAAC BROWN
BISHOP, SETH D. TO SUSAN? J. HOLLAND 12-30-1853 (1-1-1854)
BISHOP?, CEPHINEY ANN TO ARCHIBALD RAY
BLACK, ALTHA SUSAN TO JAMES E. KNUCKLES
BLACK, H. M. TO ELIZABETH COFFEE 2-23-1853 (2-24-1853)
BLACKBOURN, JACOB TO EMELINE SUTTLE 4-8-1854
BLACKBURN, LUCY ANN TO WM. P. ROBERTS
BLACKBURN, MICHAEL TO POLLY ANN PERRY 9-7-1852
BLACKBURN, PHILIP TO ELIZABETH USSEREY 1-3-1856
BLACKBURN, TELITHA ANN TO JOHN P. HOLLAND
BLACKBURNE, ALFRED TO JANE PERRY 11-20-1862 (11-24-1862)
BLACKWELL, DAVID TO MANERVA KEEF 2-20-1861 (2-24-1861)
BLAIR, JOHN TO CORNELIA PARIS 7-15-1865
BLAIR, JOHN TO SARAH SMARTT 10-2-1855
BLAIR, MALINDA A. TO JOSEPH C. GREM
BLAKE, JAMES TO MARY A. DICKERSON 4-16-1853 (;4-17-1853)
BLANTON, SARAH TO EDMOND C. SPURLOCK
BOATWRIGHT, LUCINDA E. TO JOHN W. HOPKINS
BOATWRIGHT, THOMAS E. TO MARY E. RUSSELL 9-25-1855 (9-27-1855)
BODINE, CYNTHIA TO H. C. SIMPSON
BOILES, THOMAS TO SERRILDA MEDLEY 10-16-1852 (10-17-1852)
BOLEN, AARON TO MARY M. D. BEAM 5-25-1859
BOLIN, DAVID TO NANCY JOHNSON 1-7-1857 (1-8-1857)
BOLIN, E. L. TO MARY GROVE 11-10-1856 (11-13-1856)
BOLLEN, MARTHA TO JOHN NUNERY
BOLLIN, RESETTEE TO JOSEPH DURLEY
BONNER, ADAM TO LAURA RAMSEY 9-29-1865 (COL)
BONNER, ALFRED TO MELISSA GODSON 9-23-1865 (COL)
BONNER, AMERICA TO H. J. THAXTON
BONNER, ANN TO JAMES M. BELL
BONNER, CLERICA TO WM. M. THAXTON
BONNER, CYRUS TO NANCY WALLACE 9-9-1865 (COL)
BONNER, GEO. TO MARY BONNER 9-30-1865 (COL)
BONNER, GEORGE TO LUCINDA HOBBS 9-7-1859
BONNER, JOHN TO WINNIE RAMSEY 10-2-1865 (COL)
BONNER, L. C. TO W. J. SWANN
BONNER, LEWIS TO FRANCINA RAMSEY 9-18-1865 (COL)
BONNER, MARGARET TO R. N. COONARD
BONNER, MARY C. TO BENNETT BUREN
BONNER, MARY TO GEO. BONNER
BONNER, NANCY TO GILBERT WINTON
BONNER, NANCY TO JOHN WINTON
BONNER, PRUTIN TO JANE HENNESSEE 9-3-1865 (COL)
BONNERS, S. E. TO J. W. SCOTT
BORIN, MICHAEL TO PARALEE WILLIAMS 10-31-1859 (11-1-1859)
BOSS, HALE? TO ABIGALE MOFFETT 10-3-1855
BOSS, J. M. TO HANNAH DOUGLASS 1-25-1858
BOST, BETSEY ANN TO ALLEN MYERS
BOST, SELA? TO EDWARD WHITMAN
BOTHAMS, ARMSTED TO MARANDA SMITH 10-28-1856

BOULDIN, M. P. TO ADALINE CURTISS 2-1-1854
BOULER?, MOSES TO FRANCES CRIM8-9-1855
BOWERS, JOHN M. TO SARAH BANIS? 7-5-1858 (7-8-1858)
BOWERS, WILLIAM TO DELILA JANE LANCE 2-10-1860 (2-12-1860)
BOWLIN, DANIEL TO NANCY DERRYBERRY 11-18-1864 (11-20-1864)
BOWLING, TEMPY TO HENRY BRABBIN
BOYD, M. D. S. TO MARTHA KEENE 10-2-1865
BRABBIN, HENRY TO TEMPY BOWLING 12-29-1862 (1-4-1863)
BRAGG, HESTER A. TO F. M. MANICOAT
BRAGG, NANCY A. TO ISAAC ANDERSON
BRAGG, P. H. TO LOUISA CASS 1-2-1858
BRAGG, RICHARD M. TO ELIZABETH ALEXANDER 8-21-1856
BRATCHER, J. W. TO PARSETA WHEELING 12-4-1862
BRATCHER, SAML. TO CHARITY C. NEWBY 2-25-1861 (3-5-1861)
BRATCHER, SARAH TO SAML. WILKERSON
BRAWLY, GREEK TO MARTHA AN THAXTON 9-17-1860 (9-18-1860)
BRAY, LUCINDA TO LEROY BRAZEL
BRAY, MARY JANE TO JOHN EWING
BRAZEL, LEROY TO LUCINDA BRAY 11-11-1865
BRENE?, E. G. TO ALICE M. ARGO 12-2-1865 (12-3-1865)
BREWER, ELIZA TO J. RODGERS
BREWER, REBECCA JANE TO H. S. FOWLER
BRICKEY, CALVIN L. TO MARTHA E. SWANN? 2-27-1858 (3-4-1858)
BRIEN, JOSEPH C. TO MARTHA NEAL 12-17-1857
BRIEN, MANSON M. TO MARY MARTIN 5-3-1858
BRIENT, WM. M. TO NANCY SHERMAN 7-11-1856 (7-14-1856)
BRIGHT, LUCY TO URIAH Y. DRAKE
BRIGHT, M. V. TO MARY ROLAND 3-2-1859 (3-6-1859)
BRIGHT, MARY TO JOHN T. GRIBBLE
BRIGHT, MARY TO WASHINGTON DRAKE
BRIGHT, MINERVA TO T. Z. HANKINS
BRITT, JOHN C. TO SELINA J. COOPER 12-2-1854 (12-3-1854)
BRIXEY, S. C. TO W. T. SWAN
BROOKS, AMANDA J. TO JOHN T. HUFF
BROOKS, CATHARINE TO AUGUSTUS KNOX
BROOKS, DIANAH TO JACOB LYNN
BROOKS, ISAAC TO MATILDA MELTON 9-17-1856
BROOKS, PERMELIA M. TO JOHN TOSH
BROWN, ABNER TO PARILLEE DERRYBERRY 3-25-1857
BROWN, ABSOLEM TO JANE NUNNELLY 11-15-1862 (11-21-1862)
BROWN, ALEXANDER TO FRANCES BANKS 9-4-1862
BROWN, ANERINZEE? J. TO JACOB CAGLE
BROWN, CELA TO A. J. MITCHEL
BROWN, ELIZABETH TO J. Y. CAVERNESS
BROWN, ELIZABETH TO MATHIAS WAGONER
BROWN, EVALINE TO S. J. MITCHELL
BROWN, GEORGE TO CATY GWYNN 9-21-1865 (COL)
BROWN, GREEN TO MANILA OLIVER 7-22-1854 (7-23-1854)
BROWN, HENRY TO ELIZABETH BILES 2-14-1861
BROWN, ISAAC TO DELPHA THOMPSON 2-12-1861
BROWN, ISAAC TO POLLY BISHOP 6-2-1856 (6-3-1856)
BROWN, ISAAC TO SARAH BISHOP 6-2-1865
BROWN, JACKSON TO MARY CROUCH 9-18-1865 (COL)
BROWN, JAMES TO REBECA DERRYBERRY 8-1-1862 (8-4-1862)
BROWN, JOHN TO SARAH JANE SCOTT 12-5-1859
BROWN, JOHN TO M. A. LEATHERMAN? 6-17-1858
BROWN, JOHN TO POLLY ANDERSON 9-21-1854 (9-24-1854)
BROWN, JOHN TO SARAH JANE SCOTT 12-5-1858 (12-8-1858)
BROWN, JOSEPH TO PATSEY RAMSEY 9-30-1865 (COL)
BROWN, JULIA TO SANDERS DYKUS

BROWN, LEVIRA TO ISAAC RODGERS
BROWN, MARGARET E. E. TO WM. TRAMMELLE?
BROWN, MARTHA TO JOHN PATRICK
BROWN, NANCY TO WILLIS NUNNELY
BROWN, POLLY TO WM. GWYNN
BROWN, ROBERT TO NANCY WEST 5-9-1860
BROWN, ROBT. TO MATILDA LYNN 3-29-1853 (5-1-1853)
BROWN, SARAH TO JOSEPH MELTON
BROWN, SARAH TO PLEASANT HOBBS
BROWN, SELA TO BENJAMIN MCCOLLUM
BROWN, SUSAN A. TO E. K. P. REYNOLDS
BROWN, WM. TO SALLY FERN 4-28-1854 (4-30-1854)
BROWN?, ALEXANDER? TO FRANCES BANKS 9-4-1862 (9-7-1862)
BRUSTER, NANCY TO JOSEPH MANNING
BRYAN, J. L. TO S. V. RAINS 12-22-1859
BRYAN, JOHN M. TO TENNESSEE C. GILLIS 6-24-1858
BRYANT, ADRIAN TO TENNESSEE V. ROGERS 8-21-1865
BRYANT, ADRIAN? TO SARAH MCGEE 4-7-1856 (4-8-1856)
BRYANT, GEO. TO SALLY RAMSEY 10-2-1865 (COL)
BRYANT, JOEL H. TO CYTHA ANN HAMMONS 3-6-1853
BRYANT, MARTHA TO JAMES WOOTON
BULLARD, ALBERT TO EMELINE HILDRETH 1-7-1858
BURBANK, SAMUEL TO AKENA JOHNSON 3-5-1853 (3-6-1853)
BUREN, BENNETT TO MARY C. BONNER 5-18-1861 (5-19-1861)
BURGER, CHARLOTT TO HARVEY SEALS
BURKS, R. P. TO E. T. PARIS 2-14-1857 (2-17-1857)
BURKS, RICHARD TO IRENA GREEN 4-1-1863 (4-5-1863)
BURLISON, MARY D. TO MARTIN A. BEAM
BURLISON, SARAH TO THOMAS M. DODSON
BURROUGHS, THOS. F. TO NANCY A. SMALLMAN 11-5-1857
BUTLER, JESSEE M. TO L. M. JONES 1-3-1857 (1-4-1857)
BYARS, ELIZABETH TO JOHN P. TITSWORTH
BYARS, JANE TO JAMES GORDON
BYARS, MARTHA W. TO THOMAS M. TITTWORTH
BYARS, MARY TO WM. J. FENSTON
BYARS, SAMUEL H. TO ADILINE SMITH 4-24-1855
BYBEE, HANNAH TO LEWIS SETTLE
BYBEE, JEMIAH TO WATSON MARTIN
BYBEE, JOHN W. TO ELIZABETH HASH 8-13-1860 (8-16-1860)
BYBEE, JOSEPH TO MARTHA JANE TIPTON 8-20-1856 (8-26-1856)
BYBEE, MANERVA TO HIRAM MERCER
BYBEE, MARY TO G. W. ALLEY
BYBEE, PERMELIA E. TO JOHN J. GRIBLE
BYERS, D. H. TO JAMES D. EVANS
CAGLE, BENJAMINE TO LUCINDA SMITH 12-31-1860
CAGLE, E. J. TO ASA HILL
CAGLE, EMELINE TO JAMES D. KNIGHT
CAGLE, H. M. TO LAURA LOW 8-17-1860
CAGLE, H. M. TO NANCY EADES 6-2-1855
CAGLE, JACOB TO ANERINZEE? J. BROWN 12-20-1859 (12-22-1859)
CAGLE, JACOB TO SARAH M. REYNOLDS 11-13-1852 (11-15-1852)
CAGLE, JARLEY TO FRANKEY TAYLOR 4-18-1859
CAGLE, JOHN D. TO MARTHA TAYLOR 9-8-1863 (9-9-1863)
CAGLE, POLLY ANN TO WILLIAM SMITH
CAGLE, PRESTON A. TO SOUSANAH HAYNES 12-19-1856 (12-21-1856)
CAGLE, SOUSANAH TO DANIEL R. ROBERTS
CAIN, MARY P. TO JAMES CAMP
CAIN, R. E. TO LAURA M. ARMSTRONG 12-23-1865 (12-25-1865)
CALHOUN, REBECCA E. TO LEVI RODGERS
CALLENDER, ELIZABETH TO JOHN MALONE

CAMP, JAMES TO MARY P. CAIN 11-25-1854 (11-27-1854)
CAMPAIGN, JOSEPH TO MARY FUSTON 3-7-1861
CAMPAIN, MARY TO WM. C. GRIBBLE
CAMPBELL, E. H. TO HANNAH C. MULLINS 2-10-1859 (2-13-1859)
CAMPBELL, EMILY H. TO A. R. SMITH
CAMPBELL, H. J. TO F. A. E. WOOD 8-1-1862 (8-3-1862)
CAMPBELL, MALINDA J. TO GRANVILLE TUCKER
CAMPBELL, MARGARET TO NELSON SPARKMAN
CAMPBELL, TELFORD TO MARGARET N. MOORE 10-8-1857
CANTREL, FRANCIS M. TO AMERICA M. WAMACK 12-9-1854 (12-10-1854)
CANTREL, J. M. TO M. E. HANCOCK 7-9-1853 (7-10-1853)
CANTREL, TALMA? TO SARAH ANN JONES 5-24-1856 (5-25-1856)
CANTRELL, GEO. P. TO ELIZABETH MCWHERTER 10-31-1863 (11-5-1863)
CANTRELL, JACKSON TO MARTHA FERRELL 12-30-1854 (12-31-1854)
CANTRELL, JANE TO ISAAC J. VANHOOSER
CANTRELL, JANE TO JOHN STEMBRIDGE
CANTRELL, M. E. TO G. M. SMITH
CANTRELL, PETER TO ELIZABETH PURSER 11-11-1865
CANTRELL, PETER TO SARAH GREEN 5-2-1859 (5-5-1859)
CANTRELL, SARAH TO WM. R. ETTER
CANTRELL, THOMAS J. TO NANCY K. GREEN 8-16-1859
CANTRELL, WATSON TO PERLINA MCWHERTER 11-9-1858 (11-11-1858)
CANTRELL, WILLIAM TO MARY CHRISTIAN 2-27-1856 (2-28-1856)
CANTRELL, WM. TO MARY COTTON 10-24-1860 (11-1-1860)
CAPSHAW, WILLIAM TO SARAH MCKINNY 10-17-1865
CARDNELL, NANCY TO ABRAHAM DOUGLASS
CARDWELL, MARTHA A. TO GEORGE C. FOSTER
CARDWELL, THOMAS TO MILLEY DOUGLASS 3-6-1858
CARLEY, FLORA TO ABRAHAM NORTHCUT
CARTER, ABRAHAM TO SOUSAN STEPHENS 12-29-1852 (12-30-1852)
CARTER, ADELINE TO EDWIN P. HAINES
CARTER, JANE E. TO THOMAS ESTES
CARTER, LOVICY C. TO JOHN MEDLEY
CARTER, WM. B. TO MARGARET MORRISON 7-15-1854
CARTRIGHT, ADALINE TO JOHN MEYERS
CARTRIGHT, MARTHA TO GEORGE W. AKEMAN
CARTWRIGHT, COLUMBUS TO SALLY A. LAYNE 6-24-1858
CARTWRIGHT, ISAA? L. TO MARTHA JANE CHRISTIAN 2-21-1855
CARTWRIGHT, MARTHA A. TO L. B. ROGERS
CASS, LOUISA TO P. H. BRAGG
CATES, RUBEN TO SUSAN KEELE 12-4-1852 (12-5-1852)
CATH, RUFUS TO ELIZABETH HELTON 12-25-1855
CATHCART, DOVEY TO HARRISSON WOODLOE
CATHCUT, SARAH E. TO L. L. HUDSON
CATHEY, ARCHABLE F. TO SARAH E. BARRETT 10-16-1858 (10-17-1858)
CAVERNESS, J. Y. TO ELIZABETH BROWN 8-2-1859 (8-10-1859)
CENTER, ELIZABETH TO WILLIAM SLOAN
CHASTEEN, EDNEY TO B. F. NEWBERRY
CHERRY, MARY ANN TO G. W. CUNNINGHAM
CHRISTAIN, H. J. TO J. B. POTTER
CHRISTAIN, JOHN H. TO MARY JANE DUCKWORTH 1-22-1853 (1-23-1853)
CHRISTAIN, WM. T. TO HARRIETT FREEMAN 7-3-1856
CHRISTIAN, MARTHA JANE TO ISAA L. CARTWRIGHT
CHRISTIAN, MARY TO WILLIAM CANTRELL
CHRISTIAN, SAMUEL TO LOUANA SPARKMAN 8-2-1860
CHRISTIAN, SARAH TO JOHN S. BAGGARD
CHRISTIAN, WILLIAM B. TO MARGARETT TURNER 2-25-1861
CLARK, ARCHABLE TO SARAH FRITTS 3-28-1859 (4-3-1859)
CLARK, ELIZABETH TO F. M. SMITH
CLARK, ELIZABETH TO JAMES E. SIMS

CLARK, GRACY TO ELIJAH RODGERS
CLARK, ISAAC TO ELIZABETH WAMACK 9-7-1854 (9-10-1854)
CLARK, NANCY TO WILLIAM DREWRY
CLARK, SARAH TO JOSEPH W. DANIEL
CLARK, SELINA TO ALEX WEATHERFORD
CLARK, TILDA TO SAMUEL RODGERS
CLARK, WM. TO NANCY JANE SOLOMON 12-8-1853
CLARKE, CLEMENTINE TO WM. C. WORD
CLAY, LUCINDA TO THOMAS H. SCOTT
CLAY, POLLY TO E. D. WHITMAN
CLENDENIN, FRANCIS M. TO MAHALY MARTIN 1-26-1857 (1-27-1857)
CLENDENON, JAMES N. TO CATHARINE STUBBLEFIELD 1-9-1864 (1-12-1864)
CLIFT, ELIZABETH C. TO CHARLES W. STEWART
CLIFTON, MARGARETT B. TO ISAAC GOOLSBY
CLUCK?, WM. C. TO M. C. ALISON 2-25-1863 (2-27-1863)
COFFEE, ANN A. TO D. C. SMITHSON
COFFEE, ELIZABETH TO H. M. BLACK
COLLIER, M. A. TO J. D. CUMMINGS
COLLIER, MARGARET TO W. W. WALKER
COLLIER, MARY L. TO J. W. DURHAM
COLLIER, MYRA TO WILLIS W. GORD
COLLIER, SARAH ANN TO J. D. HAMILTON
COLLINS, ABIGAL TO JAMES H. FLETCHER
COLLINS, BENJAMINE TO FRANCES A. STEWART 10-14-1865 (10-15-1865)
COLLINS, MARGARET TO AARON HIGGENBOTHAM
COLVILLE, LAURA M. TO JOHN C. M. ROSS
COLVILLE, LURINA TO DAVID EDWARDS
COLVILLE, LUSK TO ELIZABETH REYNOLDS 1-28-1860
COLVILLE, M. A. TO W. H. STUBBLEFIELD
COLVILLE, SOUSAN TO J. C. RAMSEY
COMER, SAML. TO E. J. WHEELER 11-15-1858
COMPTON, JANE B. TO JAMES M. SELLERS
COOKSEY, C. L. TO L. L. FAULKNER
COONARD, R. N. TO MARGARET BONNER 10-28-1854 (10-31-1854)
COONROD, SIMON TO MARY RAMSEY 10-3-1865 (COL)
COOPER, SELINA J. TO JOHN C. BRITT
COPE, JAMES L. TO ELIZABETH PURKINS 9-17-1860
COPE, JAMES W. M. TO ELIZABETH A. FAULKNER 10-13-1860 (10-16-1860)
COPE, JASPER TO SARAH RODGERS 10-29-1853 (10-30-1853)
COPE, MARY E. TO WM. R. MORROW
COPE, RUTH JANE TO HIRAM J. KING
COPE, SARAH E. TO FELIX G. WOMACK
COPPINGER, ALEXANDER TO RACHEL PATRIC 6-15-1855
COPPINGER, DAVID TO MARGARETT MCCOLLEM 4-10-1858 (4-12-1858)
COPPINGER, JAMES TO MALINDA TATE 3-2-1859
COTTON, MARY TO WM. CANTRELL
COTTON, WM. F. TO ELIZABETH GRIBBLE 4-27-1863
COUCH, J. W. TO NANCY P. WAMACK 9-18-1857
COUCH, T. J. TO SARAH USSERY 9-18-1857
COUNTIS?, ELIZABETH TO RICHARD MCGREGOR?
COWEN, FRANCES TO HUGH LOWE
CRAIG, MARTHA A. TO ASHER ROSSETTER
CRAVEN, ISHAM Y. TO SARAH O. ANDERSON 6-28-1852 (6-27?-1852)
CRILEY?, JAMES M. TO TEMPY DODSON 1-17-1855 (1-18-1855)
CRIM, FRANCES TO MOSES BOULER?
CRIM, WM. TO RACHEAL KELLY 3-4-1855
CRIM?, JOHN H. TO HANCY C. MARTIN 8-16-1852
CRIPS, YERBY TO RURY? MASEY 9-26-1853 (9-27-1853)
CRISP, NANCY TO MYCAJAH MAZEY
CRISP, TYRE ANN TO SAMUEL HENIGER

CROSLAND, LOTTY TO JAMES C. VADAMS
CROUCH, EDMON TO PERLINA MUNCEY 8-12-1858
CROUCH, JOHN TO EMELINE A. ROYAL 4-30-1859 (5-1-1859)
CROUCH, MARY TO JACKSON BROWN
CROUCH, NANCY C. TO S. J. GIBBS
CROUCH, THOMAS TO JULIA A. SIMPSON 2-6-1856 (2-7-1856)
CROUCH, WM. H. TO NAOMI KELTON 9-16-1865
CRUISE, ELIZA TO WM. M. MOULDER
CRUISE, POLLY ANN TO WILLIAM M. PORTER
CRUISE, STEPHEN TO NANCY E. DRAKE 7-13-1859
CRUSE, STEPHEN TO NANCY WATLEY 8-14-1865
CUMMINGS, J. D. TO M. A. COLLIER 7-23-1862 (7-27-1862)
CUMMINGS, MARGARET C. TO WM. H. SIMPSON
CUMMINGS, P. J. TO J. T. HENIGER
CUMMINGS, ROSANAH TO JAMES M. MCGEE
CUMMINGS, W. C. TO M. J. JONES 12-17-1864 (12-20-1864)
CUMMINGS, WM. B.? TO ELIZABETH GROVES 4-18-1856 (4-24-1856)
CUMMINS, SIDNEY TO ELIZABETH WATH 1-13-1853 (1-15-1853)
CUNNINGHAM, AMANDA M. TO WILLIAM J. MOORE
CUNNINGHAM, EMILINE TO ALEXANDER HARRISON
CUNNINGHAM, G. H. TO MARY MILLER 11-7-1853
CUNNINGHAM, G. W. TO MARY ANN CHERRY 12-8-1862
CUNNINGHAM, GREENBERRY H. TO MARY MILLER 11-7-1853
CUNNINGHAM, HIRAM TO NANCY WRIGHT 10-2-1856
CUNNINGHAM, J. R. TO JULIA A. ADAMSON 10-8-1860
CUNNINGHAM, JOSEPH H. TO NANCY MAUN? 9-23-1852 (9-26-1852)
CUNNINGHAM, LAURA TO MICAJAH RITCHER
CUNNINGHAM, M. A. TO J. T. GARRETSON
CUNNINGHAM, MARY F. TO EDWARD WILLIAMS
CUNNINGHAM, MARY J. TO WM. H. GARRETSON
CUNNINGHAM, MARY TO BENJAMIN F. MAYO
CUNNINGHAM, MYRA P. TO ANDERSON L. HENNESSEE
CUNNINGHAM, NEAL TO TEMPY GARRETSON 10-27-1865 (COL)
CUNNINGHAM, SARAH E. TO THOMAS GRIBLE
CURTISS, ADALINE TO M. P. BOULDIN
CURTISS, WM. TO LETISHA DODSON 5-2-1854
DANIEL, JOHN C. TO NANCY A. LANCE 11-23-1864 (11-29-1864)
DANIEL, JOSEPH W. TO SARAH CLARK 3-1-1856 (3-2-1856)
DANIEL, WILLIAM L. TO SARAH J. OVERTURFF 10-4-1862 (10-5-1862)
DARDEN, JOHNATHAN W. TO NANCY H. LAYNE 1-5-1856 (1-6-1856)
DARNELL, MARY TO NEWSOM WOOLF
DAVENPORT, L. E. S. TO T. C. LANCE
DAVENPORT, WALTER TO LOUVISA DERRYBERRY 3-19-1863 (3-22-1863)
DAVIS, JEFFERSON TO MARY JOHNSON 1-9-1858
DAVIS, JOHN C. TO M. L. YOUNGBLOOD 11-30-1861
DAVIS, MALINDA TO A. E. WOMACK
DAVIS, MARY TO JAMES VAN
DAVIS, PATSEY TO SQUIRE WILSON
DAVIS, SARAH TO WILLIS WAMACK
DAVIS, WILLIAM TO CAROLINE WAMACK 9-27-1858 (9-30-1858)
DAVIS?, A. B. TO MARTHA J. WOOTON 1-11-1858
DAVIS?, SAMUEL TO EMMA E. BENNETT 11-28-1855
DEBERRY?, MICHAEL D. TO SARAH MCNEELEY 1-3-1859 (4-5-1859)
DENTON, GEORGE TO ELIZABETH WEBB 7-14-1865
DENTON, MARY TO A. D. MURPHY
DENTON, OZIAS TO SARAH MEDLEY 9-10-1858
DENTON, RUTHA TO R. D. WEBB
DENTON, SARAH TO M. L. SELLERS
DERRYBERRY, HENRY E. TO ANNEY FREEMAN 8-25-1856
DERRYBERRY, LOUVISA TO WALTER DAVENPORT

DERRYBERRY, MARY M.? TO WILLIAM S. SHOCKLEY
DERRYBERRY, NANCY TO DANIEL BOWLIN
DERRYBERRY, PARILLEE TO ABNER BROWN
DERRYBERRY, REBECCA TO JAMES BROWN
DESTON, E. F. TO LUCIE J. SMITH 1-18-1861 (1-20-1861)
DEVENPORT, E. B. TO LUCY GOIN? 10-22-1853
DEWEESE, M. V. TO C. R. SMITH
DICKERSON, MARY A. TO JAMES BLAKE
DOBBS, J. H. TO M. A. DUKE 5-31-1863
DOBKINS, AUGUSTINE B. TO AMANDA MORRISSON 7-1-1853
DOBKINS, REBECCA TO WM. SWINDLE
DODD, JAMES TO KEZIAH KERBY 8-30-1859 (9-1-1859)
DODSON, GEORGE W. TO MARTHA SMITH 8-26-1857
DODSON, ISABELLA TO NATHAN DODSON
DODSON, LAURA M. TO ELMORE C. HAYES
DODSON, LETISHA TO WM. CURTISS
DODSON, NATHAN TO ISABELLA DODSON 9-11-1865
DODSON, POLLY ANN TO JOHN DRAKE
DODSON, SARAH TO GREENBERRY MITCHEL
DODSON, TEMPEY TO JAMES M. CRILEY
DODSON, THOMAS M. TO SARAH BURLISON 8-7-1855
DODSON?, ----- TO REDDING -----
DOSS, S. P. TO NANCY MERCER 8-9-1856
DOSS, SARAH F. TO JAMES J. WITTEY
DOUGHTY, CAROLIN TO CYRUS LYTLE
DOUGHTY, MARY TO JAS. M. NORTHCUT
DOUGLASS, ABRAHAM TO NANCY CARDNELL 12-11-1858 (12-12-1858)
DOUGLASS, H. J. TO SILAS R. YORK
DOUGLASS, HANNAH TO J. M. BOSS
DOUGLASS, JOSEPH TO ELIZABETH NEAL 2-14-1855 (2-15-1855)
DOUGLASS, M. TO A. M. ENGLAND 10-27-1863
DOUGLASS, MARTHA TO CLAYBORN GWINN
DOUGLASS, MILLEY TO THOMAS CARDWELL
DRAKE, J. V. TO H. T. FORREST
DRAKE, JOHN TO POLLY ANN DODSON 11-20-1855
DRAKE, MALVINA TO DANIEL GREEN
DRAKE, NANCY E. TO STEPHEN CRUISE
DRAKE, REUBEN M. TO MARTHA MCGEE 2-3-1856
DRAKE, SARAH ANN TO J. S. MOFFET
DRAKE, URIAH Y. TO LUCY BRIGHT 1-9-1856
DRAKE, WASHINGTON TO MARY BRIGHT 7-3-1857 (7-4-1857)
DREWRY, WILLIAM TO NANCY CLARK 8-19-1857
DUCKWORTH, MARY JANE TO JOHN H. CHRISTAIN
DUKE, M. A. TO J. H. DOBBS
DUKE, NANCY M. TO JAMES M. SIMPSON
DULNANEY, J. M. TO MARTHA J. ROLAND 12-30-1858 (1-4-1859)
DUNCAN, WM. TO NANCY ELKINS 2-10-1863 (2-12-1863)
DUNCAN, Y. D. TO MARY RICHARDSON 5-19-1856 (5-25-1856)
DUNHAM, NANCY TO JAMES C. STANLY
DUNLAP, LUTHER TO MARTHA WILSON 1-8-1865
DURHAM, J. W. TO MARY L. COLLIER 4-2-1857
DURHAM, JAMES A. TO RUTHA A. WYNNES 11-27-1852 (11-30-1852)
DURLEY, ELIJAH TO RACHEL SMARTT 9-14-1865 (COL)
DURLEY, ELIZA TO GRANDERSON JONES
DURLEY, HARRIET J. TO ELLIS NORTHCUT
DURLEY, JOSEPH TO RESETTEE BOLLIN 9-15-1865
DURLEY, MARY TO WASHINGTON SAVAGE
DURLEY, MULDA TO EDMUND RAMSEY
DURLEY, SAML. TO NANCY LARKIN 9-16-1865 (COL)
DURLEY, VIOLET TO ARNTON HAMMONS

DYANS?, ENOCH TO JANE MORTON 3-30-1854 (3-31-1854)
DYER, JOEL TO NANCY JANE MCDANIEL 8-16-1854
DYKES, ISHAM TO ELIZABETH TATE 10-31-1865
DYKUS, SANDERS TO JULIA BROWN 6-8-1862
EADES, NANCY TO H. M. CAGLE
EADY, JANE TO CHARLES MOFFETT
EADY, NANCY TO THOS. MCGAW?
EADY, SARAH C. TO BENJAMINE M. ROWLAND
EARLES, ANN E. TO WILLIAM JOHNSON
EASTWOOD, JOHN TO REBECCA SEVER 8-24-1852 (8-9?-1852)
EDGE, MARTHA TO G. P. MARTIN
EDGE, ROBERT TO MARY HAWKINS 1-7-1856 (1-10-1856)
EDINGTON, MARY TO CROCKET QUALLS
EDINGTON, TOMAS J. TO LOUIZA BESS 6-8-1854
EDWARDS, DAVID TO LURINA COLVILLE 8-4-1856 (8-5-1856)
EDWARDS, SIDNY F. TO SARAH E. SNIPS 6-7-1856
ELAM, LOUISA E. TO E. S. WALDON
ELAM, RODISA TO WM. M. FRENCH
ELAM, SAROAH TO DAVID TODD
ELKINS, M. E. TO WM. E. GRIBBLE
ELKINS, NANCY TO WM. DUNCAN
ELLIS, JANE TO JAMES ALLEN
ELLIS, M. W. TO WM. B. JOHNSON
ELLIS, MARYE? TO W. J. WILLIAMS
ELLIS, SOLAMON TO REBECCA WEBB 10-25-1853
ELLIS, TELITHA TO DOCTOR WILKERSON
ELLISON, WILLIAM TO SARAH E. RODGERS 11-23-1859
ELROD, ELIZABETH TO LEVI ROGERS
ELWIN, MARY TO WM. C. YOUNG
ENGLAND, A. M. TO M. DOUGLASS
ENGLAND, ALEXANDER TO MARY NEAL 6-5-1862 (6-8-1862)
ENGLAND, PERNETA TO JOHN N. MYERS
ENGLAND, SCOTHA TO ELIJAH D. SCOTT
EPPERSON, JOHN L. TO LIDIA C. FORREST 12-13-1856 (12-14-1856)
ESCUE, G. G. L. TO SOUSAN J. VANHOOZER 11-22-1859 (11-23-1859)
ESCUE, W. J. TO LOUISA STOGSTILL 1-25-1859 (2-1-1859)
ESTES, THOMAS TO JANE E. CARTER 12-16-1854 (12-14-1854)
ETTER, MARY TO SAMUEL A. MCKNIGHT
ETTER, MARY TO SAMUEL MCKNIGHT
ETTER, RISIN TO SARAH ANN RUTLEDGE 1-5-1859
ETTER, WM. R. TO SARAH CANTRELL 7-26-1853
EVANS, ARCHABALD TO CATHARINE ORRICK 11-10-1860 (11-11-1860)
EVANS, COLUMBIA TO JOSEPH QUICK
EVANS, J. P. TO SARAH E. MCDANIEL 1-8-1866 (1-11-1866)
EVANS, JAMES D. TO D. H. BYERS 12-6-1852 (12-7-1852)
EVANS, JAMES M. TO LOURANA SMITH 8-6-1854
EVANS, MANDAH TO JERRY JACO
EVANS, SAML. H. TO NANCY OUTLAW 12-22-1860 (12-25-1860)
EWING, JOHN TO MARY JANE BRAY 11-9-1855 (11-11-1855)
FAR, JAMES TO MARTHA ANN JONES 4-9-1862 (4-10-1862)
FARLEY, NANCY E. TO W. T. YOUNGBLOOD
FARMER, THOMAS TO REBECCA HARIMAN 8-9-1859 (8-11-1859)
FAULKNER, ADELINE TO THOMAS B. RUST
FAULKNER, ASA TO SALLY REYNOLDS 10-23-1852 (10-25-1852)
FAULKNER, ELIZABETH A. TO JAMES W. M. COPE
FAULKNER, JAMES H. TO ELIZABETH WEBB 11-8-1860
FAULKNER, L. L. TO C. L. COOKSEY 2-19-1859 (2-20-1859)
FAULKNER, M. K. TO G. C. PENNYBAKER
FAULKNER, MALISA TO L. J. MAGNESS
FAUSETT, M. E. TO J. B. WITTEY

FAUXTON, WM. H. TO NANCY ANN SCOTT 1-19-1853
FENSTON, WM. J. TO MARY BYARS 7-29-1855
FERIS, JOSEPH TO HANNAH L. READ 4-12-1855
FERN, SALLY TO WM. BROWN
FERRELL, ELIZA TO ALEX. HILDRETH
FERRELL, JESSE R. TO LUCY A. B. RAMSEY 1-11-1855
FERRELL, JOHN TO ANN A. SANDERS 10-20-1863
FERRELL, MARTHA TO JACKSON CANTRELL
FERRELL, SARAH TO S. A. J. MANGUM
FINGER, CHARLES TO MARY ANN FINGER 9-11-1865
FINGER, J. M. TO JESSE HILL
FINGER, MALINDA TO ISAAC TURNEY
FINGER, MARY ANN TO CHARLES FINGER
FINGER, MARY E. TO JAMES A. WHEELER
FISHER, ELIZABETH TO WM. J. HILL
FISHER, NARSISA TO JOEL PERRY
FLETCHER, JAMES H. TO ABIGAL COLLINS 1-27-1857
FLETCHER, POLLY TO A. J. SMITH
FLOURNOY, JULIA TO WILLIAM RIVERS
FLYNN, DENNIS TO JANE HOPKINS 9-18-1862
FORESTER, WM. J. TO SARAH K. NEAL 3-5-1856
FORREST, H. T. TO J. V. DRAKE 7-23-1864 (7-28-1864)
FORREST, LIDIA C. TO JOHN L. EPPERSON
FORREST, S. A. TO A. J. SAFLEY
FORRISTER, ELIZABETH V. TO JOHN F. GOODWIN
FOSTER, CHARLES TO REBECCA BISHOP 12-31-1857
FOSTER, GEORGE C. TO MARTHA A. CARDWELL 10-29-1853 (10-30-1853)
FOSTER, REBECCA TO THOS. J. WOOD
FOSTER?, JONATHAN TO RACHEL PASSON 5-26-1855 (5-29-1855)
FOURTON, JANE TO THOS. MCGUIRE
FOUSTON, JAMES A. TO LOUISA SANDERS 3-13-1856 (3-14-1856)
FOUSTON, PAIRLEE ANN TO FRANCIS YORK
FOUSTON, R. J. TO MARY JANE WHITE 3-12-1860
FOUSTON, SARAH TO FRANCIS MASON
FOWLER, H. S. TO REBECCA JANE BREWER 7-10-1860
FOWLER, JULI ANN TO ROBERT L. MORROW
FOWLER, LAURA M. TO SAMUEL STILES
FOWLER, MARY TO JAMES SMITH
FRAZER, JANE TO E. R. SNIDER
FREEMAN, ANNEY TO HENRY E. DERRYBERRY
FREEMAN, ELIZABETH TO DAVID A. JACOBS
FREEMAN, HARRIETT TO WM. T. CHRISTAIN
FREEMAN, MARY TO W. R. MARTIN
FREEMAN, SARAH TO JAMES WHITLOCK
FREEMAN, WM. TO LERINA STOCKSTILL 12-24-1858 (12-26-1858)
FREEMAN, WM. TO NANCY VANHOOZER 4-22-1853
FRENCH, WM. M. TO RODISA ELAM 5-28-1855 (5-31-1855)
FRESHOF, JAMES W. TO SARAH JANE JENNINGS 4-5-1856
FRITTS, SARAH TO ARCHABLE CLARK
FULTON, NANCY TO JOHN WAMACK
FULTS, CLABERRY TO SARAH STUBLEFIELD 10-9-1855
FULTS, DANIEL TO MARTHA STYLES 9-18-1854 (9-21-1854)
FULTS, DANIEL TO SARAH GREEN 8-26-1853
FULTS, ELIHUE TO MARY MCDANIEL 1-3-1855 (1-4-1855)
FULTS, HENRY TO NANCY MARTIN 2-27-1863 (3-3-1863)
FULTS, LUZANA TO WESLEY HOBBS
FURREN, JOSEPH TO HANNAH L. RADD 4-12-1855
FURREN, SYRENA TO JAMES MCDOW
FURREW, JOSEPH TO HANAH L. RAD 4-12-1855
FUSTON, J. F. TO LUIZEY LOWERY 1-9-1861 (1-10-1861)

FUSTON, MARGERETT TO GEO. W. MILLER
FUSTON, MARY TO JOSEPH CAMPAIGN
FUSTON, R. J. TO MARY J. WHITE 6-14-1860
GARDENER, W. H. TO SALLIE A. HOODENPYLE 9-18-1861
GARNER, JAMES H. TO ELIZABETH MURPHEY 2-6-1854 (2-9-1854)
GARNER, JAMES H. TO ELIZABETH LYTLE 2-6-1854
GARNER, MARGARET A. TO JAMES B. SAIN
GARRETSON, J. T. TO M. A. CUNNINGHAM 4-2-1860 (4-5-1860)
GARRETSON, TEMPY TO NEAL CUNNINGHAM
GARRETSON, WM. H. TO MARY J. CUNNINGHAM 8-20-1859 (8-23-1859)
GARTH, J. T. TO MARY C. SNEPS? 11-2-1852 (11-4-1852)
GIBBS, ELIZABETH TO JAMES M. PACE
GIBBS, ELIZABETH TO JOHN PEPPER
GIBBS, ISAAC M. TO DOVE NUNLEY 7-15-1865
GIBBS, JOHN TO DRUCILLA ARMSTRONG 11-20-1852
GIBBS, JOHN TO ELLEN MASON 10-7-1861
GIBBS, JULY D. TO GEO. W. WEBB
GIBBS, S. J. TO NANCY C. CROUCH 1-28-1859 (1-29-1859)
GIBSON, NANCY TO F. M. BARKSDALE
GILLENTINE, MALVINA TO AUDLEY WISEMAN
GILLEY, JOHN W. TO M. J. WILSON 1-23-1862
GILLEY, SIMEON TO ELIZABETH KERBY 6-21-1861 (6-23-1861)
GILLIS, TENNESSEE C. TO JOHN M. BRYAN
GIVINS, WILLIAM TO JUDA F. WALKER 1-17-1861
GLASSAY, ELIZABETH TO JAMES M. HART
GODDON, EDMUN TO ANGELINE GRIBLE 5-12-1854 (5-14-1854)
GODSON, MELISSA TO ALFRED BONNER
GOFF, A. C. TO MARY NEALY 10-31-1853 (11-2-1853)
GOIN?, LUCY TO E. B. DEVENPORT
GOOD, R. J. TO E. A. LANCE 12-8-1859
GOODRAN, JOHN TO MANDY LANE 3-15-1856 (3-16-1856)
GOODSON, JOSEPH TO TILITHA MARTIN 6-30-1856
GOODSON, NANCY TO JOHN M. WAMACK
GOODWIN, JAMES D. MARY KEITH 5-14-1856
GOODWIN, JOHN F. TO ELIZABETH V. FORRISTER 7-24-1852 (7-25-1852)
GOODWIN, WILLIAM A. TO ELIZABETH KIEF 8-30-1858 (9-1-1858)
GOODWIN, WM. TO JANE SOAPE? 9-13-1854
GOOLSBY, ISAAC TO MARGARETT B. CLIFTON 3-30-1861
GORD, WILLIS W. TO MYRA COLLIER 11-25-1862
GORDON, JAMES TO JANE BYARS 1-8-1853
GRAHAM, ELIZABETH T. TO J. C. PUTMAN
GRAHAM, MARTHA R. TO SAMUEL G. SMART
GRANT, JAMES TO ELIZABETH SHUMATE? 2-?-1857
GRAVES, MARY TO GEORGE AKINSON
GRAVITT, FIELDING TO MOXY MACON 8-6-1859
GREEN, ALCEY E. TO JOHN SULLENS
GREEN, DANIEL TO MALVINA DRAKE 1-23-1860
GREEN, ELIZABETH TO JEREMIAH WHITMAN
GREEN, HARRIET L. TO J. D. WALLING
GREEN, IRENA TO RICHARD BURKS
GREEN, JOHN TO SARAH MEADOWS 7-16-1859 (7-17-1859)
GREEN, LUCINDA TO WILLIAM LAWSON
GREEN, MARTHA TO JOHN PERRY
GREEN, MARY TO JAMES WARREN
GREEN, N. J. TO W. H. LAURENCE
GREEN, NANCY A. TO S. R. MITCHELL
GREEN, NANCY K. TO THOMAS J. CANTRELL
GREEN, SARAH E. TO JOHN T. GRIBLE
GREEN, SARAH TO DANIEL FULTS
GREEN, SARAH TO PETER CANTRELL

GREER, A. P. TO P. A. H. RIGGS 1-5-1863
GREER, ANN TO F. D. HARWELL
GREGORY, JAMES P. TO SARAH WILKERSON 6-5-1863
GREM, JOSEPH C. TO MALINDA A. BLAIR 5-19-1853
GRIBBLE CARLEE TO W. D. MOFFITT
GRIBBLE, A. J. TO SARAH A. KEEF 7-5-1860
GRIBBLE, A. P. TO MELVINA SMITH 11-1-1858 (11-7-1858)
GRIBBLE, ELIZABETH TO MATTISON S. MILLER
GRIBBLE, ELIZABETH TO WM. F. COTTON
GRIBBLE, G. W. TO S. M. HANKINS 1-11-1864
GRIBBLE, HANNAH TO D. B. SMITH
GRIBBLE, JOHN T. TO MARY BRIGHT 8-19-1863
GRIBBLE, M. V. TO MIRA H. WOODWARD 8-3-1865
GRIBBLE, MARGARET J. TO R. R. ROWLAND
GRIBBLE, SARAH E. TO JOHN F. SIMPSON
GRIBBLE, TURY? TO JAMES SWINDLE
GRIBBLE, WM. C. TO MARY CAMPAIN 6-8-1855 (6-10-1855)
GRIBBLE, WM. E. TO M. E. ELKINS 12-12-1865 (12-13-1865)
GRIBLE, A. J. TO ELIZABETH ROWLAND 2-2-1857 (2-5-1857)
GRIBLE, ANGELINE TO EDMUN GODDON
GRIBLE, G. M. TO SARAH ANN ROWLAND 10-9-1856
GRIBLE, HANNAH M. TO MACOM H. WOODWARDS
GRIBLE, JAMES S. TO CYMANTHIA WEBB 7-11-1857 (7-14-1857)
GRIBLE, JOHN J. TO PERMELIA E. BYBEE 3-13-1860 (3-15-1860)
GRIBLE, JOHN T. TO SARAH E. GREEN 12-13-1859 (12-20-1859)
GRIBLE, MANERVA TO FRANCIS NUNNELEY
GRIBLE, MARY JANE TO A. J. SMITH
GRIBLE, THOMAS TO SARAH E. CUNNINGHAM 10-1-1856
GRIFFIN, JOHN C. TO PHEREBA MELTON 7-7-1858
GRISWOLD, NORMAN W. TO ELIZA JANE SMALLMAN 6-13-1856 (6-17-1856)
GROSE, JONAH TO RACHEL MOFFETT 4-13-1854 (4-12?-1854)
GROVE, ELLEN TO THOMAS HENNESSEE
GROVE, MARY TO E. L. BOLIN
GROVES, ELIZABETH TO WM. B.? CUMMINGS
GUEST, ELIZA TO JAMES AKIN
GUNTER, F. F. TO ASBERRY MCAFEE
GUYNN, JULIA TO T. E. MABERRY
GUYNN, M. J. TO DAVID WOOTTON
GWINN, CLAYBORN TO MARTHA DOUGLASS 12-23-1852
GWINN, JASPER TO BARBARRY VANHOOSER 2-14-1854
GWYN, HARRIET TO TENNESSEE KING
GWYNN, CATY TO GEORGE BROWN
GWYNN, POLLY TO SHADRACH GWYNN
GWYNN, SHADRACH TO POLLY GWYNN 9-26-1865
GWYNN, WM. TO POLLY BROWN 9-30-1865 (COL)
HAGGARD, J. R. TO PERMELIA S. RANDOLPH 11-13-1855
HAINES, EDWIN P. TO ADELINE CARTER 5-9-1857
HALE, FRANK A. TO MARY A. KING 10-5-1865 (10-7-1865)
HALE, L. B. TO ELIZABETH MASON 11-16-1861 (11-17-1861)
HALEY, ANN TO ANDERSON NORTHCUTT
HALEY, GEORGE SR. TO ANNEY JACO 3-23-1858
HALLERMAN, ADELINE TO CHARLES P. LAYNE
HALLUN, JERRIE W. TO NANCY JACOBS 8-11-1853 (8-12-1853)
HALY, VANCE ALLEN TO SARAH JACO 3-25-1857
HAMILTON, J. D. TO SARAH ANN COLLIER 10-13-1865
HAMMER, MARY F. TO THOMAS SMOOT
HAMMER, NANCY E. TO W. B. ANDERSON
HAMMONS, ARNTON TO VIOLET DURLEY 9-16-1865
HAMMONS, CYTHA ANN TO JOEL H. BRYANT
HAMPTON, MORGAN D. TO MARTHA JANE WHITE 10-10-1857

HANCOCK, M. E. TO J. M. CANTREL
HANEY, JOSEPH TO MARTHA SWANEY 3-29-1858
HANEY, MARYANN TO GEO. W. WEBB
HANKINS, S. M. TO G. W. GRIBBLE
HANKINS, T. Z. TO MINERVA BRIGHT 9-22-1865
HANNA, J. G. TO V. S. MOONEY 9-16-1855
HANNEGIN?, ESTHER TO WM. M. MCGREGER
HARDIN, GILES TO S. MATHEWS 5-17-1858 (5-19-1858)
HARGEST, MATILDA TO THOMAS J. UNDERWOOD
HARIMAN, REBECCA TO THOMAS TURNER
HARRIS, ALEXANDER TO ELIZABETH RICKMON 7-27-1854
HARRIS, GEORGE TO PHILIPNY JENNINGS 7-21-1854
HARRIS, W. P. TO ANN WARE 11-27-1860 (11-21?-1860)
HARRISON, ALEXANDER TO EMILINE CUNNINGHAM 11-5-1859 (11-8-1859)
HARRISON, ALMIRA T. TO JOHN PICKETT
HARRISON, AUDLY TO NANCY HENNESSEE 4-13-1861 (4-14-1861)
HARRISON, MARTHA TO JESSEE JENNINGS
HARRISON, MILLEY TO ISAAC HILL
HARRISON, THOS. TO MARY BELL 12-1860 (12-27-1860)
HARRISSON, JULIA TO WILLIAM JENNINGS
HART, JAMES M. TO ELIZABETH GLASSAY 1-27-1855
HARWELL, F. D. TO ANN GREER 9-14-1859 (9-15-1859)
HARWELL, MONTGOMERY B. TO LAURA A. ARGO 1-3-1860 (1-5-1860)
HASH, ELIZABETH TO JOHN W. BYBEE
HASH, LOUISA TO RICHARD SIMPSON
HASH, TABITHA TO THOMAS A. JONES
HASSA?, JULINA TO ALEXANDER WALKER
HAWKINS, MARY TO EPHRAIM F. MYERS
HAWKINS, MARY TO ROBERT EDGE
HAYES, CALHOON TO R. C. HENNESSEE 5-6-1861 (5-7-1861)
HAYES, ELIZABETH TO JESSE MARTIN
HAYES, ELMORE C. TO LAURA M. DODSON 2-2-1860 (2-3-1860)
HAYES, JOHN L. TO MARY AKEMAN 1-20-1860
HAYES, MARTIN P. TO MARY L. PARKS 11-15-1865
HAYES, NELLEY TO THOMAS HENNESSEE
HAYMAKER, ISABELLA TO HENRY MCCLURE
HAYNES, A. S. TO W. T. WATLEY
HAYNES, SOUSANAH TO PRESTON A. CAGLE
HAYNES, WILLIAM TO MAHULDAH WHITE 5-29-1858 (5-31-1858)
HAYS, MARY TO ARCHABOLD HENNESSEE
HAYWOOD, LEONADUS TO LUCY SETLE 4-13-1853
HEART, JOHN TO SOUSAN WHITLOCK 9-22-1852 (9-23-18520
HELTON, ELIZABETH TO RUFUS CATH
HENDERSON, ROBERT C. TO MANERVA N. STROUD 10-26-1860 (OR 61?) (10-28-1860)
HENDERSON, SML. TO CORA F. ARGO 2-11-1854 (2-12-1854)
HENEGAR, JANE TO HENRY YORK
HENEGAR, JOHN C. TO PERLINA YORK 11-15-1853
HENEGER, THOMAS J. TO MARY E. SMART 9-2-1858
HENIGER, J. T. TO P. J. CUMMINGS 12-3-1864 (12-8-1864)
HENIGER, SAMUEL TO TYRE ANN CRISP 10-2-1861
HENNESSEE, ANDERSON L. TO MYRA P. CUNNINGHAM 1-1-1857
HENNESSEE, ANN TO R. M. WOODS
HENNESSEE, ARCHABOLD TO MARY HAYS 12-21-1863 (12-25-1863)
HENNESSEE, ELIZA JANE TO JOHN B. THAXTON
HENNESSEE, JANE TO JOSEPH BILES
HENNESSEE, JANE TO PRUTIN BONNER (COL)
HENNESSEE, MARY F. TO WESLEY T. KIDWELL
HENNESSEE, MARY TO ALFRED A. MOOR
HENNESSEE, NANCY TO AUDLY HARRISON
HENNESSEE, R. E. TO CALHOON HAYES

HENNESSEE, THOMAS TO ELLEN GROVE 8-10-1863 (8-20-1863)
HENNESSEE, THOMAS TO NELLEY HAYES 3-10-1856
HENNESSEE, WILLIAM TO MARTHA TALLEY 1-15-1860
HERIMAN, ELIZABETH TO WILLIAM HODGE
HERNDON, HULDA TO W. B. RICKS
HERNDON, N. A. TO N. R. WILLIAMSON
HERNDON, R. W. TO MARY ANN AKERS 5-19-1860 (5-20-1860)
HERNDON, RUTHA TO ELI JONES
HICHCOCK, MISSIAN TO B. F. -----
HICKERSON, M. J. TO E. MARTIN
HICKS, ANN TO OSCAR C. HOLLAND
HICKS, BENJAMIN F. TO SARAH WEBB 3-24-1856
HICKS, ELIN TO JAMES M. KIMBLE
HICKS, JAMES TO MARTHA JANE MILLER 10-3-1855
HICKS, JOHN C. TO MARY M. LINN 6-14-1856 (RETURNED NOT ENDORSED)
HICKS, MARY E. TO JOSEPH B. MARTIN
HIGGENBOTHAM, AARON TO MARGARET COLLINS 2-11-1860
HIGGENBOTHAM, ANGELINE TO NIMROD KELL
HIGGENBOTHAM, H. B. TO MARY PENINGTON 1-7-1856
HIGGENBOTHAM, MARY JANE TO JOHN AKEMAN
HIGGINBOTHAM, H.? H.? TO MARY JANE MCGREGER 12-8-1862 (12-9-1862)
HILDRETH, ALEX. TO ELIZA FERRELL 10-2-1853
HILDRETH, EMELINE TO ALBERT BULLARD
HILL, ASA TO E. J. CAGLE 8-3-1860 (8-15-1860)
HILL, BETHIA TO WM. C. BARNES
HILL, ISAAC TO MILLEY HARRISON 4-6-1862 (4-7-1862)
HILL, JESSE TO J. M. FINGER 7-2-1860 (7-3-1860)
HILL, JOHNATHAN P. TO VISTA SCOTT 7-12-1856
HILL, SUSANNAH TO ISAAC BARNES
HILL, WM. J. TO ELIZABETH FISHER 1-5-1854
HILLER, SARAH TO WM. L. YORK
HILLIS, ELIJAH TO ADELINE MOFFETT 2-24-1857 (2-25-1857)
HIPP, JOHN V. TO CAROLINE V. LANCE 12-6-1852 (12-7-1852)
HITCHCOCK, MILLY TO ADISON PUSLY
HITSON, THOS. J. TO NANCY MORTON 12-4-1857
HOBBS, ISAAC TO ROSEANN SMITH 11-30-1857
HOBBS, JOHN TO JULLER SMITH 5-17-1858
HOBBS, LUCINDA TO GEORGE BONNER
HOBBS, PLEASANT TO SARAH BROWN 9-6-1859 (9-7-1859)
HOBBS, WESLEY TO LUZANA FULTS 5-17-1858
HODGE, WILLIAM TO ELIZABETH HERIMAN 4-21-1858
HOLDER, ROBERT TO SARAH JANE HOLDER 2-13-1857 (RETURNED WITHOUT ENDORSEMENT)
HOLDER, SARAH JANE TO ROBERT HOLDER
HOLFERD, EDMOND TO A. G. VAUGHN 4-24-1860
HOLLAND, A. C. TO SARAH C. OLIVER 10-7-1852
HOLLAND, C. A. TO M. C. SUMMERS
HOLLAND, CHARITY E. TO GEORGE W. VAUGHN
HOLLAND, JAMES B. TO FRANCES RUSSELL 7-28-1855 (7-31-1855)
HOLLAND, JANE TO JAMES JACO
HOLLAND, JOHN P. TO TELITHA ANN BLACKBURN 9-16-1854 (9-17-1854)
HOLLAND, OSCAR C. TO ANN HICKS 4-17-1859
HOLLAND, SUSAN? J. TO SETH D. BISHOP
HOLMES, G. P. TO LOUISA ANDERSON 9-14-1861 (9-15-1861)
HOLMES, ISAAC R. TO MARTHA A. MORRISSON 12-3-1853 (12-4-1853)
HOODENPYLE, MYRA TO ISHAM MARTIN
HOODENPYLE, NANCY TO LEONEDUS STUBBLEFIELD
HOODENPYLE, SALLIE A. TO W. H. GARDENER
HOPKINS, GEORGE D. TO CATHERINE STEWART 4-10-1855 (4-15-1855)
HOPKINS, HUGH F. TO MARY WILSON 8-1-1865
HOPKINS, JANE TO DENNIS FLYNN

HOPKINS, JANE TO G. W. MULLINS
HOPKINS, JOHN H. TO ALEDA RODES 9-13-1858 (9-16-1858)
HOPKINS, JOHN W. TO LUCINDA E. BOATWRIGHT 2-20-1854 (2-23-1854)
HOPPER, WILLIAM B. TO MARY ANN KOGER 10-16-1852 (10-17-1852)
HOUSTON, THOMAS J. TO NARCISSA V. STUBLEFIELD 7-18-1860 (7-19-1860)
HOWARD, J. T. TO S. J. RICKS 8-19-1861 (8-20-1861)
HUBBARD, JANE TO PHILLIP JACO
HUBBARD, LOCKEY W. TO W. S. SIMPSON
HUBBARD, MARY H. TO ZACHARIAH MARQUIS?
HUDSON, ELIJAH TO ANN ELIZA JENNINGS 1-14-1864
HUDSON, JAMES TO SARAH VANHOOSER 12-22-1858 (12-23-1858)
HUDSON, L. L. TO SARAH E. CATHCUT 2-15-1858 (2-11?-1858)
HUFF, JOHN T. TO AMANDA J. BROOKS 9-30-1857
HUGHES, AARON TO MARY WOOLDRIDGE 7-11-1862
HUGHES, PHILA ANN TO WM. SMITH
HUMBLE, SARAH J. TO J. P. BILES
HUMBLE, WM. J. TO MARY THAXTON 12-6-1852
HURNDON, CHARLOTTE TO JOHN LEICH
HUTCHISON, ELIZABETH TO WM. M. YORK
HUTSON, A. C. TO NANCY MARTIN 4-14-1853 (4-13?-1853)
HUTSON, JAMES M. TO MARTHA KOGER 9-17-1853 (9-18-1853)
JACKSON, GEORGE TO SARAH TATE 1-14-1853
JACO, ANNEY TO GEORGE HALEY SR.
JACO, JAMES TO JANE HOLLAND 3-26-1859
JACO, JERRY TO LUCINDA ADKINS 10-6-1858
JACO, JERRY TO MANDAH EVANS 1-29-1855 (1-31-1855)
JACO, PHILLIP TO JANE HUBBARD 12-21-1863
JACO, SARAH TO VANCE ALLEN HALY
JACO, URIAH TO PERCELLA M. ROWLAND 10-29-1856 (10-30-1856)
JACO, WILEY TO NANCY ADKINS 11-30-1862
JACOBS, DAVID A. TO ELIZABETH FREEMAN 4-12-1858
JACOBS, DAVID A. TO JAMES K. WHITLOCK
JACOBS, DAVID TO SAROAH PACE 8-29-1853
JACOBS, ELIZABETH TO WM. C. BARNES
JACOBS, NANCY TO JERRIE W. HALLUN
JENNINGS, ANN ELIZA TO ELIJAH HUDSON
JENNINGS, ELISHA P. TO SOUSAN A. ROWAN 9-12-1860
JENNINGS, ELIZABETH TO JOSEPH E. MCGEE
JENNINGS, JESSEE TO MARTHA HARRISON 6-7-1863
JENNINGS, PHILIPNY TO GEORGE HARRIS
JENNINGS, SARAH JANE TO JAMES W. FRESHOF
JENNINGS, WILLIAM TO JULIA HARRISSON 1-10-1857 (1-11-1857)
JOHNSON, AKENA TO SAMUEL BURBANK
JOHNSON, CYNTHIA TO ALEXANDER OVERBEY
JOHNSON, ELIZABETH TO COPPER SCOTT
JOHNSON, J.? W. TO MARY S. STUBBLEFIELD 10-3-1865
JOHNSON, MARIAH TO JULIOUS PICKETT
JOHNSON, MARY TO JEFFERSON DAVIS
JOHNSON, NANCY TO DAVID BOLIN
JOHNSON, WILLIAM TO ANN E. EARLES 9-1-1860 (9-2-1860)
JOHNSON, WM. B. TO M. W. ELLIS 11-2-1852 (11-3-1852)
JONES, ALICE TO HENDERSON SAFLEY
JONES, ANN TO RAULEIGH MARTIN
JONES, B. F. TO M. J. VICKERS 8-10-1863
JONES, ELI TO RUTHA HERNDON 12-14-1853 (12-15-1853)
JONES, ELIZABETH TO GILLUM B. MERCER
JONES, ELIZABETH TO JOSEPH WEBB
JONES, GRANDERSON TO ELIZA DURLEY 9-25-1865 (COL)
JONES, H. A. TO D. M. TRAVIS
JONES, ISAAC TO EASTHER MCGEE 9-27-1853

JONES, ISAAH TO SARAH ELIZABETH LEWIS 12-11-1855
JONES, ISABELLA TO MARSHALL ROBERTS
JONES, ISAIAH TO MARY D. MOORE 2-1-1864
JONES, J. A. TO HARRETT MARTIN 2-15-1859 (2-16-1859)
JONES, JEFFERSON TO SOUSAN E. BADGER 4-2-1855 (4-3-1855)
JONES, JOHN E. TO CATHERIN RODGERS 10-24-1859
JONES, JOSEPH L. TO FANNY B. WILSON 8-1-1860
JONES, L. C. TO SEDIANN SMITH 1-7-1856 (1-10-1856)
JONES, L. M. TO JESSEE M. BUTLER
JONES, LOUCINDA TO O. M. THURMON
JONES, LOUIZA TO W. J. VANHOOSER
JONES, M. E. TO R. A. SMITH
JONES, M. J. TO W. C. CUMMINGS
JONES, MARKE TO CHARLOTTE? RODGERS 10-14-1856
JONES, MARTHA ANN TO JAMES FAR
JONES, MARY J. TO JAMES J. ANDERSON
JONES, MARY JANE TO MELVIN DALLAS ADKINS
JONES, MATHEW JR.. TO NANCY JANE MULLICAN 12-27-1856 (12-28-1856)
JONES, SARAH ANN TO TALMA? CANTREL
JONES, SARAH JANE? TO T. J. MULLICAN
JONES, SOUSAN E. TO B. F. STROUD
JONES, SUSAN TO JAMES A. MARLOR
JONES, THOMAS A. TO TABITHA HASH 4-29-1861 (5-1-1861)
JONES, U. E. TO JULIA ANN SMITH 11-13-1855 (11-14-1855)
JONES, W. J. TO SOUSAN L. ROWAN 10-14-1858
JORDEN, JAMES TO SARAH C. MILLER 7-16-1864 (7-19-1864)
KEATHLEY, WILLIS TO MARY ANN ROBERTS 7-16-1860 (7-19-1860)
KEEF, MANERVA TO DAVID BLACKWELL
KEEF, SARAH A. TO A. J. GRIBBLE
KEELE, HARVEY H. TO CLARASY WILKERSON 12-9-1852
KEELE, SUSAN TO RUBEN CATES
KEELIN, E. G. TO MARGARETT ROGERS 11-24-1860 (11-25-1860)
KEENE, MARTHA TO M. D. S. BOYD
KEEZEY, JACOB TO ELVIRA THOMAS 10-26-1860
KEITH, MARY TO JAMES D. GOODWIN
KELL, NIMROD TO ANGELINE HIGGENBOTHAM 11-1-1860
KELLEY, PARALEE T. TO A. T. STANLEY
KELLY, RACHEAL TO WM. CRIM
KELTON, NAOMI TO WM. H. CROUCH
KELTON, R. H. TO DICEY M. TATE 3-11-1859 (3-17-1859)
KENNEDEY, THOMAS K. TO MARGARET WILSON 8-2-1858 (8-3-1858)
KENNEDY, ANNY TO KELLY ALLISON
KENT, L. D. TO MARY WAMACK 8-31-1855
KERBY, ELIZABETH TO HIRAM PARKER
KERBY, ELIZABETH TO SIMEON GILLEY
KERBY, JOHN TO DEELY RICKMAN 11-30-1860 (12-2-1860)
KERBY, KEZIAH TO JAMES DODD
KERBY, W. N. TO MARY D. MOORE 12-11-1862
KERLY, MARY M. TO DEMPSEY ROLER
KIDWELL, WESLEY T. KIDWELL TO MARY F. HENNESSEE 9-23-1865
KIEF, ELIZABETH TO WILLIAM A. GOODWIN
KIMBLE, JAMES M. TO ELIN HICKS 6-6-1855
KING, ELIZABETH TO GARY RAMSEY
KING, GILLY TO SAML. THAXTON
KING, HIRAM J. TO RUTH JANE COPE 3-22-1856 (3-23-1856)
KING, MARY A. TO FRANK A. HALE
KING, MARY E. TO JOHN H. PERRY
KING, NED TO MARTHA NORTHCUTT 9-16-1865 (COL)
KING, TENNESSEE TO HARRIET GWYN 9-30-1865 (COL)
KIRKPATRICK, J. G. TO JULIETTE C. STEBBINS 12-12-1858 (2-14-1858?)

KNIGHT, DOLPHIN TO SARAH JANE ONEAR 1-16-1854 (1-17-1854)
KNIGHT, JAMES D. TO EMELINE CAGLE 6-26-1852 (6-27-1852)
KNOX, AMANA J. TO JOHN G. RAINS
KNOX, AUGUSTUS TO CATHARINE BROOKS 7-6-1858
KNUCKLES, JAMES E. TO ALTHA SUSAN BLACK 3-2-1854
KOGER, MARTHA TO JAMES M. HUTSON
KOGER, MARY ANN TO WILLIAM B. HOPPER
KOIL, M. J. TO M. V. MARSHALL
LANCE, CAROLINE V. TO JOHN V. HIPP
LANCE, DELILA JANE TO WILLIAM BOWERS
LANCE, E. A. TO R. J. GOOD
LANCE, J. N. TO ELLEN V. TAYLOR 9-2-1865
LANCE, J. S. TO ELIZABETH BATES 12-20-1865 (12-21-1865)
LANCE, MARTHA E. TO W. W. PRATOR
LANCE, NANCY A. TO JOHN C. DANIEL
LANCE, R. E. TO J. H. BARRETT
LANCE, T. C. TO L. E. S. DAVENPORT 2-4-1859 (2-6-1859)
LANE, MANDY TO JOHN GOODRAN
LANE, W. S. TO E. P. WATTERMAN? 12-28-1856 (SB 1855; EXECUTED 12-30-1855)
LARKIN, NANCY TO SAML. DURLEY
LAURENCE, ELIZA TO ISAAC SCOTT
LAURENCE, W. H. TO N. J. GREEN 7-6-1861 (7-7-1861)
LAW, EZEKIEL TO SARAH RYONS 10-25-1856
LAWRANCE, C. T. TO CYNTHA PHILLIPS 2-13-1861
LAWRENCE, M. R. TO MANURVA SMITH 1-8-1853
LAWS?, JAMES M. TO MARY UPCHURCH 7-12-1853 (7-24-1853)
LAWSON, LYDA TO W. F. MEDLEY
LAWSON, WILLIAM TO LUCINDA GREEN 2-15-1858
LAYNE, CHARLES P. TO ADELINE HALLERMAN 8-8-1856
LAYNE, ELSBERRY TO E. B. BILES 10-28-1857
LAYNE, LEONARD TO SARAH SEWELL 11-25-1852 (11-26-1852)
LAYNE, NANCY H. TO JOHNATHAN W. DARDEN
LAYNE, SALLY A. TO COLUMBUS CARTWRIGHT
LEATHERMAN?, M. A. TO JOHN BROWN
LEICH, JOHN TO CHARLOTTE HURNDON 9-16-1853
LENNINGS, MARTHA TO C. M. MARTIN
LEWIS, SARAH ELIZABETH TO ISAAH JONES
LINN, MARY M. TO JOHN C. HICKS
LOCK, JOHN R. TO MARTHA ROSS 10-2-1856
LOCKE, RHODA TO DOLA SMARTT
LOCKHERT, JOHN W. TO CAROLINE SPRING? 3-22-1860 (4-12-1860)
LOGUE, A. G. TO MARY A. RUTLEDGE 2-25-1857
LOW, HUGH TO SARAH PORTER 8-2-1858 (8-3-1858)
LOW, LAURA TO H. M. CAGLE
LOW, MARTHA TO JAMES ADIER
LOWE, HUGH TO FRANCES COWEN 12-26-1859 (12-27-1859)
LOWE, MARY E. TO WILLIAM MITCHELL
LOWERY, LUIZEY TO J. F. FUSTON
LOWRANCE, MARGARET? TO ----- MILSTEAD
LOWRY, M. V. TO S. C. SELLERS 7-16-1860 (7-19-1860)
LOWRY, MATILDA TO OTHENIEL SWEET
LOYNE, LUENTIN T. TO LEVY E. WILHOIT
LUSK, AMY TO J. F. MORFORD
LUSK, ANN E. TO J. F. MORFORD JR
LUTHER, ISRAEL TO LESA USSERY 9-13-1858
LUTTRELL, CROCKET TO ROSA JANE SHRADER 9-8-1858 (9-16-1858)
LUVARD, WALTER B. TO JULIA F. WILCHER 9-20-1865
LYNN, ISAAC V. TO MINERVA J. WITT 12-24-1864 (12-25-1864)
LYNN, JACOB TO DIANAH BROOKS 2-25-1857 (2-26-1857)
LYNN, JACOB TO MARY LYTLE 2-23-1864 (2-24-1864)

LYNN, JAMES TO EMALINE BARRETT 1-25-1864
LYNN, MATILDA TO ROBT. BROWN
LYNN, WILLIAM TO MARTHA PARSON 3-22-1854 (3-23-1854)
LYTLE, A. J. TO C. L. NORTH 5-1-1855 (5-2-1855)
LYTLE, CYRUS TO CAROLIN DOUGHTY 3-21-1853 (3-24-1853)
LYTLE, ELIZABETH TO JAMES H. GARNER
LYTLE, MARY TO JACOB LYNN
MABERRY, T. E. TO JULIA GUYNN 11-23-1859 (11-24-1859)
MACON, ELIZABETH J. TO H. J. H. J. TAYLOR
MACON, JOHN TO MARTHA ANN RAMSEY 12-8-1855 (12-9-1855)
MACON, JOSEPH K. TO N. J. WINDHAM 2-22-1865
MACON, MOXY TO FIELDING GRAVITT
MACON, ROMULUS TO E. J. STYLES 2-28-1859
MADEWELL, WILLIAM TO MARY MCCOLLUM 7-18-1859 (7-19-1859)
MADUX, E. A. TO J. M. ALEXANDER
MAGNESS, L. J. TO MALISA FAULKNER 11-11-1857
MALONE, JOHN TO ELIZABETH CALLENDER 4-3-1856
MANGUM, ELENOR TO WM. K. SLOAN
MANGUM, MARY JANE TO JOHN L. SLOAN
MANGUM, S. A. J. TO SARAH FERRELL 1-29-1856 (1-30-1856)
MANICOAT, F. M. TO HESTER A. BRAGG 10-25-1863
MANNING, JOSEPH TO NANCY BRUSTER 3-2-1859
MANNING, NANCY TO SAMUEL ALLS
MANNING, WILLIAM R. TO SOUSAN RANKHORN 8-29-1858
MANSFIELD, ELIZABETH TO SILUS RODGERS
MARBERRY, P. H. TO M. E. SCOTT 10-14-1858
MARCOMB, S. B. TO MARGARETT J. BIFORD 2-10-1839
MARCOMB, S. B. TO MARGARTT J. BIFORD 2-10-1859
MARCUM, MARTHA TO O. D. MULLICAN
MARLER, REBECCA TO JAMES NEWLY
MARLOR, JAMES A. TO SUSAN JONES 3-11-1856 (3-13-1856)
MARQUIS?, ZACHARIAH TO MARY H. HUBBARD 8-23-1853 (8-25-1853)
MARSHALL, M. V. TO M. J. KOIL 9-20-1860
MARSHALL, THOMAS TO ESTHER WILSON 7-7-1853
MARTIN, C. M. TO MARTHA LENNINGS 2-20-1859 (2-25-1859)
MARTIN, CATHARINE TO JOHN TEPLES
MARTIN, E. TO M. J. HICKERSON 9-6-1861 (9-5?-1861)
MARTIN, ELIZABETH J. TO F. M. MOFFITT
MARTIN, G. P. TO MARTHA EDGE 2-9-1853 (2-11-1853)
MARTIN, HANCY C. TO JOHN H. CRIM
MARTIN, HARRETT TO J. A. JONES
MARTIN, ISHAM TO MYRA HOODENPYLE 11-15-1858 (11-17-1858)
MARTIN, JAMES L. TO ELLEN VICKERS 2-4-1860 (2-5-1860)
MARTIN, JESSE TO ELIZABETH HAYES 6-22-1854 (6-27-1854)
MARTIN, JOHN TO MARTHA ANN ADCOCK 8-31-1857
MARTIN, JOSEPH B. TO MARY E. HICKS 3-10-1853 (3-11-1853)
MARTIN, L. A. TO A. D. THORP
MARTIN, LAUSON TO MARY ANN WARE 12-1-1859
MARTIN, LOUIZA JANE TO WM. ALLEN
MARTIN, MAHALY TO FRANCIS M. CLENDENIN
MARTIN, MARTHA P. TO LYMAN B. MCCRARY
MARTIN, MARY TO J. M. WILKERSON
MARTIN, MARY TO MANSON M. BRIEN
MARTIN, NANCY TO A. C. HUTSON
MARTIN, NANCY TO HENRY FULTS
MARTIN, R. A. TO SARAH MOLDER 7-14-1863
MARTIN, RAULEIGH TO ANN JONES 12-6-1855 (12-7-1855)
MARTIN, TILITHA TO JOSEPH GOODSON
MARTIN, W. R. TO MARY FREEMAN 10-1-1860 (10-7-1860)
MARTIN, WATSON A.? TO JEMIAH BYBEE 10-13-1855 (10-17-1855)

MARTIN, WM. W. L. TO MARY ANN BANES 8-13-1853 (8-17-1853)
MARTON?, CHARLES TO ABBYGALE MOFFETT 4-25-1860
MASE, ELIZABETH TO JAMES WILSON
MASEY, RURY? TO YERBY CRIPS
MASEY, S. A. TO CATHARINE MILLER 1-23-1864 (1-24-1864)
MASON, ELIZABETH TO L. B. HALE
MASON, ELLEN TO JOHN GIBBS
MASON, FRANCIS TO SARAH FOUSTON 5-27-1856
MASON, MARY TO DAVID OWEN
MASON, MARY TO JAMES WYMAN?
MASTON, BETSEY TO JESSEE WILSON
MATHEWS, C. S. TO J. A. BILES
MATHEWS, CAROLINE TO JOHN NORTHCUT
MATHEWS, J. C. TO A. A. AKERS 10-25-1859
MATHEWS, JOHN C. TO NANCY C. PATTEN 6-5-1857
MATHEWS, LOUZETTER TO D. A. STROUD
MATHEWS, M. J. TO J. L. RHEA
MATHEWS, MARTHA TO HENRY RHEA
MATHEWS, S. TO GILES HARDIN
MAUN?, NANCY TO JOSEPH H. CUNNINGHAM
MAYFIELD, ADAM TO MARTHA ANN BARNES 10-23-1862 (10-26-1862)
MAYFIELD, ELIZABETH TO JAMES MAYSE
MAYFIELD, JULIAN TO GEORGE MAYZE
MAYFIELD, MARGARETT TO WILLIAM SIMONS
MAYFIELD, POLLY TO ROBERT SIMONS
MAYO, BENJAMIN F. TO MARY CUNNINGHAM 12-18-1858 (12-19-1858)
MAYO, ELIZA JANE TO WM. M. MOULDER
MAYO, GEORGE TO SALLY PURSLY 5-15-1858
MAYSE, JAMES TO ELIZABETH MAYFIELD 7-23-1858 (7-27-1858)
MAYSEY, MARY TO W. H. RUSSELL
MAYSEY, MIRA TO ELIJAH WOODLEE
MAYZE, GEORGE TO JULIAN MAYFIELD 6-7-1856 (6-8-1856)
MAZEY, MYCAJAH TO NANCY CRISP 8-18-1859 (8-21-1859)
MCAFEE, ASBERRY TO F. F. GUNTER 10-11-1862
MCAFEE, BILBRA TO F. E. PATEY 9-25-1865
MCBRIDE, ELMIRA TO WM. M. ROACH
MCCLURE, HENRY TO ISABELLA HAYMAKER 10-6-1865
MCCOLLEM, MARGARETT TO DAVID COPPINGER
MCCOLLUM, BENJAMIN TO SELA BROWN 3-25-1858
MCCOLLUM, MARY TO JOHN H. SAMPLES
MCCOLLUM, MARY TO WILLIAM MADEWELL
MCCORKLE, EMALINE TO DANIEL OREAR
MCCRARY, LYMAN B. TO MARTHA P. MARTIN 2-28-1856
MCDANIEL, C. A. TO MARGARET WILLIAMS 8-4-1859
MCDANIEL, EDWARD TO LUCINDA -ANKHAM 7-28-1862
MCDANIEL, FRANK TO MALETTA ADCOCK 9-22-1862
MCDANIEL, G. W. TO LEVINA TIPTON 11-6-1862
MCDANIEL, J. C. TO FRANCES A. TAYLOR 9-15-1863 (9-16-1863)
MCDANIEL, JAMES TO MARY WILSON 2-18-1861
MCDANIEL, LUCINDA TO E. J. WRIGHT
MCDANIEL, LYDIA TO ISAIAH SHOCKLY
MCDANIEL, MARTHA J. TO HEUSTON MEYERS
MCDANIEL, MARY TO ELIHUE FULTS
MCDANIEL, NANCY JANE TO JOEL DER
MCDANIEL, RHODA TO BENJAMINE MERIS
MCDANIEL, SARAH E. TO J. P. EVANS
MCDANIEL, WILLIAM TO ELIZABETH A. RIGGS 11-23-1858
MCDARNELD, MARY ANN TO TRACEK TOSH?
MCDOUGAL, JANE TO JAMES STYLES
MCDOW, JAMES TO SYRENA FURREN 4-25-1854 (4-29-1854)

MCDOWEL, FRANK TO MARY ADKINS 4-23-1859 (4-24-1859)
MCDOWELL, FRANK TO MALETTA ADCOCK 11-18-1862
MCGAW?, THOS. TO NANCY EADY 12-25-1858
MCGEE, ARCHABALD TO LOUISA BESS 9-27-1864 (9-29-1864)
MCGEE, EASTHER TO ISAAC JONES
MCGEE, JAMES M. TO ROSANAH CUMMINGS 1-12-1860
MCGEE, JOSEPH E. TO ELIZABETH JENNINGS 6-15-1856
MCGEE, MANERVA TO JOHN A. STEPP
MCGEE, MARTHA TO REUBEN M. DRAKE
MCGEE, MARTIN TO ELIZABETH WISEMAN 11-2-1855
MCGEE, MARY ANN TO JAMES M. TEMPLETON
MCGEE, NANCY J. TO WILLIAM C. STEPP
MCGEE, POLLY ANN TO JOHN PATRICK
MCGEHEE, BENJAMINE TO ANN WOOTON 9-25-1865 (COL)
MCGEHEE, BETTY TO WESLEY WOOTON
MCGHEE, SARAH TO ADRIAN? BRYANT
MCGREGER, CLINTON TO MELCENA MYERS 11-16-1852 (11-18-1852)
MCGREGER, MARY JANE TO H.? H.? HIGGINBOTHAM
MCGREGER, WM. W. TO ESTHER HANNEGIN? 7-11-1855
MCGREGOR, MARY JANE TO JAMES D. TATE
MCGREGOR?, RICHARD TO ELIZABETH COUNTIS? 4-11-1862 (4-12-1862)
MCGRUGER, TABITHA TO WM. RODGERS
MCGUIRE, JOHN W. TO LOUISA SEALS 7-19-1953
MCGUIRE, THOS. TO JANE FOURTON 10-25-1853 (10-26-1853)
MCHERNDON, R. HENRY TO AMERICA E. RAINS 11-12-1859
MCINTURFF, J. M. TO ELIZA C. SIMS 5-1-1860 (5-5-1860)
MCKINNY, SARAH TO WILLIAM CAPSHAW
MCKNIGHT, MARY TO JOHN L. WOODLEY
MCKNIGHT, SAMUEL A. TO MARY ETTER 7-13-1854 (7-14-1853?)
MCKNIGHT, SAMUEL TO MARY ETTER 7-13-1853
MCLANE, ELIZABETH C. TO L. S. RAY
MCLENELL?, MARY E. TO WM. D. WALLACE
MCMAHAN, WILLIAM TO EMILINE ALEXANDER 3-15-1855 (3-22-1855)
MCNEELEY, J. H. TO MARY ANN STANLEY 3-12-1859 (3-15-1859)
MCNEELEY, SARAH TO MICHAEL DEBERRY?
MCNELEY, RODY H. TO JOSEPH SMITH
MCPHERUN, NANCY TO ELIAS WEBB
MCWHERTER, ELIZABETH TO GEO. P. CANTRELL
MCWHERTER, PERLINA TO WATSON CANTRELL
MCWHORTER, SARAH R. TO TELFORD STEWART
MEADOWS, SARAH TO JOHN GREEN
MEDDOWS, JOHN TO JULA ANN PERRY 8-23-1863 (8-24-1863)
MEDLEY, G. W. TO DIDEMY? WEBB 11-5-1859 (11-6-1859)
MEDLEY, GREEN TO MARGARET SMITH 12-20-1865
MEDLEY, JOHN TO LOVICY C. CARTER 6-6-1861
MEDLEY, LUISA E. TO P. S. POWELL
MEDLEY, NANCY A. TO JOHN WILEY
MEDLEY, SARAH TO OZIAS DENTON
MEDLEY, SERRILDA TO THOMAS BOILES
MEDLEY, W. F. TO LYDA LAWSON 11-17-1862
MEEKER, JENNIE TO WILEY WEBSTER
MELTON, JOSEPH TO SARAH BROWN 3-29-1858
MELTON, M. E. TO P. H. PLEMONS
MELTON, MATILDA TO ISAAC BROOKS
MELTON, NAOMA TO L. C. PLEMONS
MELTON, PHEREBA TO JOHN C. GRIFFIN
MERCER, GILLUM B. TO ELIZABETH JONES 10-30-1854 (11-2-1854)
MERCER, HIRAM TO MANERVA BYBEE 10-13-1860
MERCER, NANCY TO S. P. DOSS
MERIS?, BENJAMINE TO RHODA MCDANIEL 11-1-1859

Warren County, Tennessee, Marriages 1852-1865

MERRIWETHER, NILES TO L. P. SMITH 10-24-1855 (10-25-1855)
MEYERS, HEUSTON TO MARTHA J. MCDANIEL 7-31-1865 (8-3-1865)
MEYERS, JOHN TO ADALINE CARTRIGHT 4-15-1862 (4-17-1862)
MILLER, CATHARINE TO S. A. MASEY
MILLER, GEO. W. TO MARGERETT FUSTON 12-19-1860 (12-21-1860)
MILLER, MAHALA TO FRANCIS M. BARKER
MILLER, MARTHA JANE TO JAMES HICKS
MILLER, MARY TO G. H. CUNNINGHAM
MILLER, MARY TO GREENBERRY H. CUNNINGHAM
MILLER, MATTISON S. TO ELIZABETH GRIBBLE 8-31-1865
MILLER, NANCY ANN TO M. B. SPARKMAN
MILLER, SARAH C. TO JAMES JORDEN
MILSTEAD, ----- TO MARGARET? LOWRANCE 9-30-1859
MITCHEL, A. J. TO CELA BROWN 1-1-1855
MITCHEL, GREENBERRY TO SARAH DODSON 9-18-1857
MITCHELL, DAVID L. TO ELIZABETH SKELTON 11-29-1854
MITCHELL, JUDAH TO WILLIAM C. WILLIS
MITCHELL, R. M. TO W. C. SANDERS
MITCHELL, S. J. TO EVALINE BRON 12-30-1852 (1-2-1853)
MITCHELL, S. R. TO NANCY A. GREEN 11-23-1857
MITCHELL, WILLIAM TO MARY E. LOWE 9-23-1863
MOFFET, AARON TO ELIZABETH SMITH 2-17-1853
MOFFET, J. S. TO SARAH ANN DRAKE 10-23-1865 (10-29-1865)
MOFFET, MALINDA E. TO J. N. ROWLAND
MOFFETT, ABBYGALE TO CHARLES MARTON?
MOFFETT, ABIGALE TO HALE? BOSS
MOFFETT, ADELINE TO ELIJAH HILLIS
MOFFETT, CHARLES TO JANE EADY 12-8-1853
MOFFETT, RACHEL TO JONAH GROSE
MOFFIT, F. A. L. J. TO P. F. MYERS
MOFFITT, F. M. TO ELIZABETH J. MARTIN 10-24-1865
MOFFITT, W. D. TO CARLEE GRIBBLE 10-14-1865
MOHLER, J. G. TO MARTHA B. SULLIVAN 11-16-1865
MOLDER, SARAH TO R. A. MARTIN
MOODY, LEWIS TO MALINDA SHIPMAN? 6-29-1857 (7-1-1857)
MOONEY, V. S. TO J. G. HANNA
MOORE, ALFRED A. TO MARY HENNESSEE 11-16-1859 (11-17-1859)
MOORE, MARGARET N. TO TELFORD CAMPBELL
MOORE, MARY D. TO ISAIAH JONES
MOORE, MARY D. TO W. N. KERBY
MOORE, WILLIAM J. TO AMANDA M. CUNNINGHAM 12-13-1859 (12-15-1859)
MORFORD, J. F. JR. TO ANN E. LUSK 1-4-1854
MORFORD, J. F. TO AMY LUSK 1-4-1854 (SB 1855? IS WITH 1855 RETURNS)
MORGAN, EZEKIEL TO NANCY A. TAYLOR 8-2-1854
MORRISON, MARGARET TO WM. B. CARTER
MORRISSON, AMANDA TO AUGUSTINE B. DOBKINS
MORRISSON, MARTHA A. TO ISAAC R. HOLMES
MORROW, ELIZABETH TO ROBERT STYLES
MORROW, ROBERT L. TO JULI ANN FOWLER 5-19-1858
MORROW, WM. R. TO MARY E. COPE 9-9-1865
MORTON, JANE TO ENOCH DYANS?
MORTON, MARY W. TO M. R. M. SMITH
MORTON, NANCY TO THOS. J. HITSON
MOULDER, ELIZABETH TO A. J. SMITH
MOULDER, WM. M. TO ELIZA CRUISE 7-22-1862 (7-24-1862)
MOULDER, WM. M. TO ELIZA JANE MAYO 9-12-1859 (9-14-1859)
MULLICAN, FRANCES TO THOMAS BESS
MULLICAN, NANCY ANN TO ABRAM POTTER
MULLICAN, NANCY JANE TO MATHEW JONES JR.
MULLICAN, O. D. TO MARTHA MARCUM 10-26-1863

MULLICAN, T. J. TO SARAH JANE? JONES 4-18-1863
MULLICAN, WILLIAM W. TO ELVIRA A. POTTER 7-22-1864 (7-24-1864)
MULLIN, JOHN TO KATHARINE WHITLOCK 4-4-1859 (4-7-1859)
MULLINS, G. W. TO JANE HOPKINS 7-5-1853
MULLINS, HANNAH C. TO E. H. CAMPBELL
MUNCEY, PERLINA TO EDMON CROUCH
MURFREE, CAROLINE TO D. H. WOODLEE
MURPHEY, C. C. TO ELIZA TOWLES 8-16-1855
MURPHEY, ELIZABETH TO JAMES H. GARNER
MURPHY, A. D. TO MARY DENTON 9-19-1863
MYERS, ALLEN TO BETSEY ANN BOST 9-15-1855
MYERS, EPHRAIM F. TO MARY HAWKINS 8-23-1855
MYERS, JOHN A. TO PERNETA ENGLAND 10-15-1855 (10-16-1855)
MYERS, MELCENA TO CLINTON MCGREGOR
MYERS, P. F. TO F. A. L. J. MOFFITT 12-17-1862
MYERS, P. M. TO SARAH A. BILES 7-17-1858
NEAL, ELIZABETH TO JOSEPH DOUGLASS
NEAL, HANNAH TO JEREMIAH BELL
NEAL, MARTHA TO JOSEPH C. BRIEN
NEAL, MARY TO ALEXANDER ENGLAND
NEAL, SARAH K. TO WM. J. FORESTER
NEALY, MARY TO A. C. GOFF
NEBLETT, THURSA A. TO JAMES A. SNIPES
NEBLETT, WM. TO THURSDAY A. WARE 4-27-1857 (4-28-1857)
NELSON, ANGELINA G. TO GEORGE STROUD
NEWBERRY, E. F. TO EDNEY CHASTEEN 12-13-1862
NEWBY, CHARITY C. TO SAML. BRATCHER
NEWBY, HANNAH TO EULYSSES VANHOOSER
NEWBY, SUSAN J. TO DAVID SMITH
NEWLY, G. A. M. TO SARAH WHEELER 12-23-1854 (12-27-1854)
NEWLY, JAMES TO REBECCA MARLER 7-12-1854 (7-15-1854)
NEWLY, WM. TO MARY STEWART 10-1-1853
NICHOLS, W. C. TO COLUMBIA N. TAYLOR 1-12-1864
NORTH, C. L. TO A. J. LYTLE
NORTH, WM. H. TO E. C. WATERS 4-20-1855
NORTHCUT, ABRAHAM TO FLORA CARLEY 9-17-1865 (COL)
NORTHCUT, ELLIS TO HARRIET J. DURLEY 9-16-1865 (COL)
NORTHCUT, ISAAC TO PHILA ANN STOTTS 1-2-1855 (1-3-1855)
NORTHCUT, JAS. M. TO MARY DOUGHTY 12-30-1854 (1-1-1855)
NORTHCUT, JOHN TO CAROLINE MATHEWS 10-9-1857
NORTHCUTT, ANDERSON TO ANN HALEY 1-25-1864 (1-28-1864)
NORTHCUTT, MARTHA TO NED KING
NORTHCUTT, MARTHA TO WM. ORRICK
NORTHCUTT, MARY A. TO A. D. WHEELER
NORTON, M. TO SARAH RAINS 9-14-1861 (9-16-1861)
NUNERY, JOHN TO MARTHA BOLLEN 8-29-1854 (8-30-1854)
NUNLEY, DOVE TO ISAAC M. GIBBS
NUNLEY, MILLEY TO Z. H. SKURLOCK
NUNNELEY, CAROLINE TO JAMES R. WARD
NUNNELEY, FRANCIS TO MANERVA GRIBLE 7-14-1859
NUNNELLY, ARCHABLE TO BETSEY ANN PAYNE 9-1-1860 (9-2-1860)
NUNNELLY, G. W. TO ANN ROGERS 8-22-1863
NUNNELY, JANE TO ABSOLEM BROWN
NUNNELY, ROSANAH TO R. B. SKELTON
NUNNELY, WILLIS TO NANCY BROWN 10-3-1859 (10-9-1859)
ODEL, BETHEL TO SARAH M. MANERVA RICHARDSON 9-17-1857
OLIVER, M. S. TO MELVINA SHELTON 9-8-1853
OLIVER, MANILA TO GREEN BROWN
OLIVER, SARAH C. TO A. C. HOLLAND
ONEAL, AMANDA TO JOHN M. PATTON

ONEAL, KING TO NANCY C. RAWLINGS 1-17-1853
ONEAR, SARAH JANE TO DOLPHON KNIGHT
OREAR?, DANIEL TO EMALINE MCCORKLE 3-29-1856 (3-21?-1856)
ORRICK, CATHARINE TO ARCHABALD EVANS
ORRICK, T. E. TO M. A. RICKETTS 11-30-1860 (12-2-1860)
ORRICK, VIRGINIA E. TO OBEDIAH WOOD
ORRICK, WM. TO MARTHA NORTHCUTT 6-7-1856 (6-8-1856)
OUTLAW, NANCY TO SAML. H. EVANS
OVERBEY, ALEXANDER TO CYNTHIA JOHNSON 4-24-1858
OVERTURFF, MARGARET TO JEFFERSON TURNER
OVERTURFF, MARY TO JOHN L. ROBERTS
OVERTURFF, SARAH J. TO WILLIAM L. DANIEL
OWEN, DAVID TO MARY MASON 9-28-1854
OWENS, MELVINA TO JOHN TOUHY
PACE, JAMES M. TO ELIZABETH GIBBS 11-22-1858 (11-23-1858)
PACE, SAROAH TO DAVID JACOBS
PAINE, MARIAH E. TO J. W. POINDEXTER
PARIS, CORNELIA TO JOHN BLAIR
PARIS, E. T. TO R. P. BURKS
PARKER, HIRAM TO ELIZABETH KERBY 4-6-1857 (4-8-1857)
PARKER, PHEBA TO EDWIN RUDNICK
PARKS, MARY L. TO MARTIN P. HAYS
PARSON, MARTHA TO WILLIAM LYNN
PASSON, RACHEL TO JONATHAN FOSTER?
PATEY, F. E. TO BILBRA MCAFEE
PATRIC, RACHEL TO ALEXANDER COPPINGER
PATRICK, JOHN TO MARTHA BROWN 12-3-1863 (12-6-1863)
PATRICK, JOHN TO POLLY ANN MCGEE 3-5-1857
PATTEN, NANCY C. TO JOHN C. MATHEWS
PATTERSON, ELIZABETH TO ALFRED WALLING
PATTON, ANDREW S. TO ELIZABETH SMITH 10-4-1859
PATTON, J. T. TO CYNTHA SAFLEY 2-2-1864
PATTON, JOHN M. TO AMANDA ONEAL 12-12-1865
PATY, LUISA J. TO G. T. SAINE
PAYNE, BETSEY ANN TO ARCHABLE NUNNELLY
PEAK, LUCY TO FURMAN SMARTT
PEAY, RACHEL TO CARY STROUD
PENINGTON, MARY TO H. B. HIGGENBOTHAM
PENNIBAKER, S. P. TO H. J. STONE 3-13-1861
PENNINGTON, CALEB TO NANCY WEBB 8-25-1856
PENNINGTON, ORREN TO EMELINA SMITH 10-8-1854
PENNINGTON, W. J. TO DIDAMA WEBB 10-4-1860
PENNYBAKER, G. C. TO M. K. FAULKNER 12-24-1852 (1-27-1853)
PEPPER, AARON A. TO CLEMENTINE ALLISON 10-3-1856
PEPPER, CLEMENTINE TO JOSEPH C. TALLY
PEPPER, JOHN TO ELIZABETH GIBBS 8-24-1861
PEPPER, WM. S. TO CYNTHIA ADISON 8-10-1864 (8-11-1864)
PERRY, JANE TO ALFRED BLACKBURNE
PERRY, JOEL TO NARSISA FISHER 12-6-1862 (12-8-1862)
PERRY, JOHN H. TO MARY E. KING 9-19-1865
PERRY, JOHN TO MARTHA GREEN 1-27-1864 (2-4-1864)
PERRY, JULA ANN TO JOHN MEDDOWS
PERRY, POLLY ANN TO MICHAEL BLACKBURN
PHILIPS, J. H. TO ELIZABETH WARREN 6-15-1865
PHILLIPS, CYNTHA TO C. T. LAWRANCE
PICKETT, JOHN TO ALMIRA T. HARRISON 2-23-1854
PICKETT, JULIOUS TO MARIAH JOHNSON 7-28-1860
PITTS, RODA TO KULS? WHITLOCK
PLEMONS, L. C. TO NAOMA MELTON 5-21-1856 (5-25-1856)
PLEMONS, P. H. TO M. E. MELTON 4-1-1854 (4-2-1854)

POE, ELIJAH TO MARTHA T. POE 11-11-1853
POE, MARTHA T. TO ELIJAH POE
POINDEXTER, J. W. TO MARIAH E. PAINE 12-23-1852 (1-23-1853)
POPE, MARY J. TO WM. H. WHITE
PORTER, SARAH TO HUGH LOW
PORTER, WILLIAM M. TO POLLY ANN CRUISE 7-30-1859 (7-31-1859)
POTTER, ABRAM TO NANCY ANN MULLICAN 3-6-1861
POTTER, ELVIRA TO WILLIAM W. MULLICAN
POTTER, J. B. TO H. J. CHRISTAIN 11-25-1854 (11-26-1854)
POTTER, RICHARD TO SARAH BELL 10-21-1865
POTTER, WILLIAM A. TO MARTHA TITSWORTH 7-14-1860 (7-16-1860)
POWELL, ALEXANDER TO SARAH STROUD 3-17-1858
POWELL, HARRIETT TO M. S. STROUD
POWELL, MARTHA ANN TO JAMES H. TALLEY
POWELL, P. S. TO LUISA E. MEDLEY 4-20-1861 (4-21-1861)
PRATER, LETTY ANN TO W. H. WALLACE
PRATOR, W. W. TO MARTHA E. LANCE 1-13-1863
PRICE, MALINDA J. TO ELI J. SUMMERS
PURKINS, ELIZABETH TO JAMES L. COPE
PURSER, ELIZABETH TO PETER CANTRELL
PURSLEY, ALEXANDER TO HARRIETT SMITH 7-17-1858 (7-18-1858)
PURSLY, SALLY TO GEORGE MAYO
PUSLY, ADISON TO MILLY HITCHCOCK 1-25-1859
PUTMAN, J. C. TO ELIZABETH T. GRAHAM 2-1-1855
QUALLS, CROCKET TO MARY EDINGTON 4-24-1858
QUALLS, ELIZA ELIZABETH TO JACKSON QUALLS
QUALLS, JACKSON TO ELIZA ELIZABETH QUALLS 3-18-1859
QUICK, ANN TO WM. TEMPLETON
QUICK, JACKSON TO REBECCA TEMPLETON 8-27-1855
QUICK, JOSEPH TO COLUMBIA EVANS 9-11-1865
RAD, HANAH L. TO JOSEPH FURREW
RADD, HANNAH L. TO JOSEPH FURREN
RAHM, HENRY TO SELINA RIGGS 1-30-1862
RAINS, ALBERT TO MARTHA ARGO 9-23-1865 (COL)
RAINS, AMERICA E. TO R. HENRY MCHERNDON
RAINS, HANNAH TO ALLEN SNELLING
RAINS, JOHN G. TO AMANA J. KNOX 11-1-1856 (11-4-1856)
RAINS, S. V. TO J. L. BRYAN
RAINS, SARAH TO M. NORTON
RAINS, THOMAS TO ELIZABETH WILSON 12-22-1858 (12-23-1858)
RAMSEY, ANICA TO COOPER STROUD
RAMSEY, BETTY TO SANDY RAMSEY
RAMSEY, EDMUND TO MULDA DURLEY 9-15-1865 (COL)
RAMSEY, FRANCINA TO LEWIS BONNER
RAMSEY, GARY TO ELIZABETH KING 3-25-1857 (3-26-1857)
RAMSEY, ISAAC TO MARTHA RAMSEY 9-19-1865 (COL)
RAMSEY, J. C. TO SOUSAN COLVILLE 1-29-1853 (2-1-1853)
RAMSEY, LAURA TO ADAM BONNER
RAMSEY, LUCY A. B. TO JESSE R. FERRELL
RAMSEY, LUCY TO POMPEY RAMSEY
RAMSEY, MARTHA ANN TO JOHN MACON
RAMSEY, MARTHA TO ISAAC RAMSEY
RAMSEY, MARY TO SIMON COONROD
RAMSEY, PATSEY TO JOSEPH BROWN
RAMSEY, POMPEY TO LUCY RAMSEY 10-2-1865 (COL)
RAMSEY, S. M. TO MARTHA SMARTT 2-22-1858
RAMSEY, SALLY TO GEO. BRYANT
RAMSEY, SAML. TO SARAH WHEELER 9-25-1865 (COL)
RAMSEY, SAMUEL M. TO OCTAVIA SMARTT 6-19-1853 (6-23-1853)
RAMSEY, SANDY TO BETTY RAMSEY 10-2-1865 (COL)

RAMSEY, WINNIE TO JOHN BONNER
RAMSEY, WM. TO MARY TAYLOR 3-4-1861 (3-6-1861)
RANDOLPH, ANDERSON TO MARY STILES 6-18-1856 (6-19-1856)
RANDOLPH, LETITIA TO REUBIN ROBERTS
RANDOLPH, PERMELIA S. TO J. R. HAGGARD
RANDOLPH, WILEY C. TO JULIA M. STYLES 9-10-1856 (9-11-1856)
RANKHORN, SOUSAN TO WILLIAM R. MANNING
RASCO, J. R. TO L. F. BATES 1-3-1859 (1-16-1859)
RAWLINGS, NANCY C. TO KING ONEAL
RAY, ARCHIBALD TO CEPHINEY ANN BISHOP? 11-2-1854
RAY, L. S. TO ELIZABETH C. MCLANE 11-17-1863 (11-20-1863)
REACE, REBECCA TO JONATHAN WATERHOUSE
READ, HANNAH L. TO JOSEPH FERIS
READER, GEORGE W. TO AVEY WILSON 9-7-1852
REED, ESTHER L.? TO ALLEN WARE
REEDER, MARY S. TO JOSEPH M. SHERRELL
REEDER, ROSANAH TO JAMES WILSON
REEDER, ROSANAH TO WILLIAM E. TAYLOR
REYNOLDS, E. K. P. TO SUSAN A. BROWN 11-30-1861 (12-1-1861)
REYNOLDS, E. P. TO SARAH A. ROACH 3-23-1860 (3-25-1860)
REYNOLDS, ELIZABETH TO LUSK COLVILLE
REYNOLDS, SALLY TO ASA FAULKNER
REYNOLDS, SARAH M. TO JACOB CAGLE
RHEA, ADAM TO ESTHER S. WEBB 3-3-1856 (3-5-1856)
RHEA, ARCHD. TO EUPHEMEA ANN BISHOP 11-21-1854 (WITH 1853 ENTRIES)
RHEA, HENRY TO MARTHA MATHEWS 12-30-1865 (12-31-1865)
RHEA, ISAAC TO NANCY BESS 5-2-1860 (5-3-1860)
RHEA, J. L. TO M. J. MATHEWS 5-2-1863
RHEA, ROBERT H. TO ROSANER B. WOODS 1-12-1861 (1-13-1861)
RHEA, WILLIAM TO MARGARETT A. SAIN 12-1-1865 (12-3-1865)
RICHARDSON, DAVID TO MARY ANN WORLEY 2-16-1859 (2-17-1859)
RICHARDSON, MARY TO Y. D. DUNCAN
RICHARDSON, SARAH M. MANERVA TO BETHEL ODEL
RICKETTS, M. A. TO T. E. ORRICK
RICKMAN, DEELY TO JOHN KERBY
RICKMON, ELIZABETH TO ALEXANDER HARRIS
RICKS, S J. TO J. T. HOWARD
RICKS, W. B. TO HULDA HERNDON 10-13-1860 (10-14-1860)
RIDE?, DAVID TO DELPHA STONER 7-14-1859
RIGGS, ELIZABETH A. TO WILLIAMMCDANIEL
RIGGS, P. A. H. TO A. P. GREER
RIGGS, SELINA TO HENRY RAHM
RITCHER, MICAJAH TO LAURA CUNNINGHAM 6-17-1854
RIVERS, WILLIAM TO JULIA FLOURNOY 12-28-1857
ROACH, SARAH A. TO E. P. REYNOLDS
ROACH, WM. M. TO ELMIRA MCBRIDE 1-10-1856
ROBERSON, JOSEPH H. TO SARAH J. SHOCKLEY 2-17-1859
ROBERSON, M. B. TO HANNAH E. WITTEY 1-23-1857
ROBERSON, MARY R. TO THOS. SMITH
ROBERSON, T. C. TO NANCY TODD 2-4-1857 (2-5-1857)
ROBERTS, DANIEL R. TO SOUSANAH CAGLE 10-12-1855
ROBERTS, JAMES M. TO JULETT? ADCOCK 10-25-1862 (10-26-1862)
ROBERTS, JOHN L. TO MARY OVERTURFF 12-17-1853
ROBERTS, MARGARETT E. TO LOD ROWLAND
ROBERTS, MARSHALL TO ISABELLA JONES 9-1-1860
ROBERTS, MARY ANN TO WILLIS KEATHLEY
ROBERTS, REUBIN TO LATITIA RANDOLPH 9-22-1865
ROBERTS, SEMERAL M. TO LOUIZA J. BELL 8-28-1855
ROBERTS, THOMAS TO MELISSA SPURLOCK 9-1-1865
ROBERTS, W. D. TO LUCINDA BELL 12-10-1856

ROBERTS, WM. P. TO LUCY ANN BLACKBURN 3-31-1853
ROBERTSON, BERNULA? A. TO D. L. SHOCKLEY
RODES, ALEDA TO JOHN H. HOPKINS
RODES, ELIZABETH TO PHILIP SHOCKLEY
RODES, J. HENRY TO ALIDA W. SNOWDEN 12-18-1855 (12-20-1855)
RODES, WM. TO ELIZABETH A. ROLLINS 5-24-1854
RODGERS, CATHERIN TO JOHN E. JONES
RODGERS, CHARLOTTE? TO MARKE JONES
RODGERS, ELIJAH TO GRACY CLARK 8-2-1857
RODGERS, ISAAC TO LEVIRA BROWN 10-13-1853
RODGERS, ISAIAH TO SARAH WEBB 9-27-1854
RODGERS, J. TO ELIZA BREWER 10-13-1853
RODGERS, JOHN TO ELIZABETH ROSS 8-17-1853
RODGERS, LEVI TO REBECCA E. CALHOUN 3-28-1857
RODGERS, SAMUEL TO ELIZABETH SOLOMON 10-16-1853
RODGERS, SAMUEL TO TILDA CLARK 8-31-1857
RODGERS, SARAH E. TO WILLIAM ELLISON
RODGERS, SARAH TO JASPER COPE
RODGERS, SILUS TO ELIZABETH MANSFIELD 2-16-1859 (2-17-1859)
RODGERS, WM. TO TABITHA MCGRUGER 7-18-1854
ROGERS, ANN TO G. W. NUNNELLY
ROGERS, L. B. TO MARTHA A. CARTWRIGHT 8-24-1863 (8-25-1863)
ROGERS, LEVI TO ELIZABETH ELROD 8-17-1865
ROGERS, MARGARETT TO E. G. KEELIN
ROGERS, TENNESSEE V. TO ADRIAN BRYANT
ROLAND, MARTHA J. TO J. M. DULNANEY
ROLAND, MARY TO M. V. BRIGHT
ROLER, DEMPSEY TO MARY M. KERLY 12-29-1856 (12-30-1856)
ROLLINS, ELIZABETH A. TO WM. RODES
ROSS, ELIZABETH TO JOHN RODGERS
ROSS, JOHN C. M. TO LAURA M. COLVILLE 6-12-1861
ROSS, MARTHA TO JOHN R. LOCK
ROSSETTER, ASHER TO MARTHA A. CRAIG 2-16-1856 (2-15?-1856)
ROWAN, SOUSAN A. TO ELISHA P. JENNINGS
ROWAN, SOUSAN L. TO W. J. JONES
ROWEN, LITITIA TO JOHN STILES
ROWLAND, BENJAMINE M. TO SARAH C. EADY 3-15-1858
ROWLAND, ELIZABETH TO A. J. GRIBLE
ROWLAND, J. N. TO MALINDA E. MOFFET 10-21-1853
ROWLAND, JAMES TO MARTHA C. WILKERSON 8-17-1853
ROWLAND, LOD TO MARGARETT E. ROBERTS 4-6-1863
ROWLAND, PERCELLA M. TO URIAH JACO
ROWLAND, R. R. TO MARGARET J. GRIBBLE 11-25-1852
ROWLAND, SARAH ANN TO G. M. GRIBLE
ROWLAND, WM. C. TO MARTHA UPCHURCH 10-28-1852
ROYAL, EMELINE A. TO JOHN CROUCH
ROYAL, JOHN H. TO SARAH WHITE 12-19-1857
RUDNICK?, EDWIN TO PHEBA PARKER 10-14-1854 (10-16-1854)
RUSHING, CALVIN TO MARY RUSHING 9-29-1865 (COL)
RUSHING, MARY TO CALVIN RUSHING
RUSIN?, MARGRET B. TO J. W. SEPHINS
RUSSELL, FRANCES TO JAMES B. HOLLAND
RUSSELL, MARY E. TO THOMAS E. BOATWRIGHT
RUSSELL, W. H. TO MARY MAYSEY 11-30-1854
RUST, THOMAS B. TO ADELINE FAULKNER 4-10-1854
RUTLEDGE, MARY A. TO A. G. LOGUE
RUTLEDGE, NANCY TO JOSEPH WAGANER
RUTLEDGE, SARAH ANN TO RISIN ETTER
RYONS, SARAH TO EZEKIEL LAW
SAFELY, A. J. TO S. A. FORREST 9-24-1860 (9-21?-1860)

SAFELY, ELIZABETH TO J. T. SIMS
SAFLEY, CYNTHA TO J. T. PATTON
SAFLEY, HENDERSON TO ALICE JONES 3-15-1864 (3-20-1864)
SAIN, JAMES B. TO MARGARET A. GARNER 11-1-1858 (11-4-1858)
SAIN, MARGARETT A. TO WILLIAM RHEA
SAINE, G. T. TO LUISA J. PATY 2-13-1861
SAMPLES, JOHN H. TO MARY MCCOLLUM 2-4-1856
SANDERS, ANN A. TO JOHN FERRELL
SANDERS, LOUISA TO JAMES A. FOUSTON
SANDERS, W. C. TO R. M. MITCHELL 11-16-1858 (11-18-1858)
SAPP, WM. S. TO FRANCES C. STRAUBE 8-1-1853
SAVAGE, GEORGE M. TO NANCY JANE WILSON 6-2-1854
SAVAGE, JEFFERSON TO CAROLINE TURNER 12-30-1855
SAVAGE, JESSEE TO MYRA WILLIAMS 5-31-1858
SAVAGE, JOSEPHINE C. TO WILLIAM D. SMARTT
SAVAGE, WASHINGTON TO MARY DURLEY 9-15-1865 (COL)
SCOTT, COPPER TO ELIZABETH JOHNSON 2-28-1854 (2-29-1854)
SCOTT, ELIJAH D. TO SCOTHA ENGLAND 11-25-1858
SCOTT, ISAAC TO ELIZA LAURENCE 1-12-1860
SCOTT, J. W. TO S. E. BONNERS 5-14-1855 (5-15-1855)
SCOTT, LOUCINDA TO ELI SCOTT?
SCOTT, M. E. TO P. H. MARGERRY
SCOTT, NANCY ANN TO WM. H. FAUXTON
SCOTT, SARAH JANE TO JOHN BROWN
SCOTT, SARAH JANE TO JOHN BROWN
SCOTT, THOMAS H. TO LUCINDA CLAY 6-17?-1853 (6-18-1853)
SCOTT, VISTA TO JOHNATHAN P. HILL
SCOTT?, ELI TO LOUCINDA SCOTT 9-11-1853
SCOTT?, PHILA ANN TO ISAAC NORTHCUT
SEALS, HARVEY TO CHARLOTT BURGER 9-17-1853 (9-23-1853)
SEALS, LOUISA TO JOHN W. MCGUIRE
SEALS, MARGARET TO M. C. BANKS
SEALS, MARY ANN TO GEORGE C. SORELL
SELLERS, EUDORA M. TO C. C. WILSON
SELLERS, JAMES M. TO JANE B. COMPTON 7-19-1856 (7-23-1856)
SELLERS, M. L. TO SARAH DENTON 1-8-1859 (1-9-1859)
SELLERS, S. C. TO M. V. LOWRY
SELLERS, WILLIAM TO RHODA WHERLEY 9-7-1859
SEPHINS, J. W. TO MARGRET B. RUSIN? 3-5-1855 (3-7-1855)
SETLE, LUCY TO LEONADUS HAYWOOD
SETLER, MILDRED TO P. M. WADE
SETTLE, LEWIS TO HANNAH BYBEE 8-24-1865 (COL)
SEVER, REBECCA TO JOHN EASTWOOD
SEWELL, SARAH TO LEONARD LAYNE
SHELTON, MELVINA TO M. S. OLIVER
SHERMAN, NANCY TO WM. M. BRIENT
SHERRELL, JOSEPH M. TO MARY S. REEDER 1-21-1861
SHERRELL, M. M. TO MARY ALLISON 11-17-1860
SHIPMAN?, MALINDA TO LEWIS MOODY
SHOCKLEY, D. L. TO BERNULA? A. ROBERTSON 1-4-1858 (1-7-1858)
SHOCKLEY, PHILIP TO ELIZABETH RODES 11-30-1853 (12-1-1853)
SHOCKLEY, SARAH J. TO JOSEPH H. ROBERSON
SHOCKLEY, WILLIAM S. TO MARY M.? DERRYBERRY 9-26-1856 (9-28-1856)
SHOCKLY, ISAIAH TO LYDIA MCDANIEL 4-12-1864 (4-13-1864)
SHRADER, ROSA JANE TO CROCKET LUTTRELL
SHRADER, SARAH TO WILLIAM H. BELL
SHUMATE?, ELIZABETH TO JAMES GRANT
SIMONS, ROBERT TO POLLY MAYFIELD 2-14-1856
SIMONS, WILLIAM TO MARGARETT MAYFIELD 1-13-1862 (1-14-1861)
SIMPSON, H. C. TO CYNTHIA BODINE 12-19-1864 (12-21-1864)

SIMPSON, JAMES M. TO NANCY M. DUKE 1-18-1855
SIMPSON, JOHN F. TO SARAH E. GRIBBLE 11-13-1865
SIMPSON, JULIA A. TO THOMAS CROUCH
SIMPSON, RICHARD TO LOUISA HASH 7-6-1860 (7-8-1860)
SIMPSON, RUFUS TO MELVINA WOMACK 9-17-1860 (9-18-1860)
SIMPSON, W. S. TO LOCKEY W. HUBBARD 5-1-1863
SIMPSON, WM. H. TO MARGARET C. CUMMINGS 11-13-1865
SIMS, ELIZA C. TO J. M. MCINTURFF
SIMS, J. T. TO ELIZABETH SAFELY 6-14-1853
SIMS, JAMES E. TO ELIZABETH CLARK 4-23-1859 (5-18-1859)
SISSOM, JOHN A. TO NANCY M. THAXTON 11-11-1861 (11-12-1861)
SKELTON, ELIZABETH TO DAVID L. MITCHELL
SKELTON, R. B. TO ROSANAH NUNNELEY 6-29-1858
SKURLOCK, Z. H. TO MILLEY NUNLEY 12-3-1853 (12-4-1853)
SLOAN, JOHN L. TO MARY JANE MANGUM 1-29-1856
SLOAN, WILLIAM TO ELIZABETH CENTER 10-29-1856
SLOAN, WM. K. TO ELENOR MANGUM 1-23-1856
SMALLMAN, ELIZA JANE TO NORMAN W. GRISWOLD
SMALLMAN, NANCY A. TO THOS. F. BURROUGHS
SMALLMAN, S. M. TO JOSEPH W. TAYLOR
SMART, MARY E. TO THOMAS J. HENEGER
SMART, SAMUEL G. TO MARTHA R. GRAHAM 4-3-1855
SMARTT, DOLA TO RHODA LOCKE 9-16-1865 (COL)
SMARTT, FURMAN TO LUCY PEAK 9-30-1865
SMARTT, JAMES P. TO MARY A. SMITH 9-30-1856
SMARTT, JOSEPHINE A. TO JAMES M. SPURLOCK
SMARTT, LARRY TO MARIA TRAVIS 8-27-1865 (COL)
SMARTT, MARTHA TO PETER SMARTT
SMARTT, MARTHA TO S. M. RAMSEY
SMARTT, OCTAVIA TO SAMUEL M. RAMSEY
SMARTT, PETER TO MARTHA SMARTT 9-30-1865 (COL)
SMARTT, RACHEL TO ELIJAH DURLEY
SMARTT, SARAH TO JOHN BLAIR
SMARTT, WETLY TO LAURA SNELLING 12-2-1865 (COL)
SMARTT, WILLIAM D. TO JOSEPHINE C. SAVAGE 5-3-1859 (5-5-1859)
SMARTT, WILLIAM T. TO HAMP THOMAS 1-21-1858
SMITH, A. J. TO ELIZABETH MOULDER 1-22-1859 (1-23-1859)
SMITH, A. J. TO MARY JANE GRIBLE 1-28-1856
SMITH, A. J. TO POLLY FLETCHER 3-1-1857
SMITH, A. R. TO EMILY H. CAMPBELL 12-4-1856 (12-7-1856)
SMITH, ADILINE TO SAMUEL H. BYARS
SMITH, C. R. TO M. V. DEWEESE 8-9-1852
SMITH, D. B. TO HANNAH GRIBBLE 9-9-1858
SMITH, DAVID TO SUSAN J. NEWBY 12-31-1860 (1-3-1861)
SMITH, ELIZABETH TO AARON MOFFET
SMITH, ELIZABETH TO ANDREW S. PATTON
SMITH, EMELINA TO ORREN PENNINGTON
SMITH, F. M. TO ELIZABETH CLARK 1-8-1861
SMITH, G. M. TO M. E. CANTRELL 6-30-1859
SMITH, GEMIMA JANE TO ALEXANDER BALLOW
SMITH, HARRIETT TO ALEXANDER PURSLEY
SMITH, J. STURT TO DIDEMA WEBB 6-7-1859
SMITH, JAMES TO MARY FOWLER 6-9-1859 (7-9-1859)
SMITH, JOSEPH TO RODY H. MCNELEY 3-28-1857 (3-29-1857)
SMITH, JULIA ANN TO U. E. JONES
SMITH, JULLER TO JOHN HOBBS
SMITH, L. P. TO NILES MERRIWETHER
SMITH, LOURANA TO JAMES M. EVANS
SMITH, LUCIE J. TO E. F. DESTON
SMITH, LUCINDA TO BENJAMINE CAGLE

SMITH, M. J. TO J. HENRY VANNERSON
SMITH, M. R. M. TO MARY W. MORTON 1-10-1857 (1-11-1857)
SMITH, MANURVA TO M. R. LAWRENCE
SMITH, MARANDA TO ARMSTED BOTHAMS
SMITH, MARGARET TO GREEN MEDLEY
SMITH, MARSHALL N. TO SARAH STEWART 5-12-1854 (5-21-1854)
SMITH, MARTHA A. B. TO RICHARD SMITH
SMITH, MARTHA F. TO W. S. BELOTE
SMITH, MARTHA TO GEORGE W. DODSON
SMITH, MARY A. TO JAMES P. SMARTT
SMITH, MARY TO LEVY WEBB
SMITH, MELVINA TO A. P. GRIBBLE
SMITH, MIRTHA? E. TO ORLANDER J. YORK
SMITH, NANCY J. TO HESEKIAH ALLEN
SMITH, PARALEE TO FRANKLIN BINKLEY
SMITH, R. A. TO M. E. JONES 10-11-1860 (10-16-1860)
SMITH, RHODA H. TO THOS. J. THOMPSON
SMITH, RICHARD TO MARTHA A. B. SMITH 8-7-1852 (8-8-1852)
SMITH, ROSEANN TO ISAAC HOBBS
SMITH, SALLIE ANN TO EDWARD YAGAR
SMITH, SEDEANN TO L. C. JONES
SMITH, THOMAS J. TO MARGARET TALLY 9-25-1854 (9-26-1854)
SMITH, THOS. TO MARY R. ROBERSON 3-17-1860 (3-18-1860)
SMITH, WILLIAM TO POLLY ANN CAGLE 3-31-1859 (4-1-1859)
SMITH, WM. TO PHILA ANN HUGHES 9-12-1854
SMITHSON, D. C. TO ANN A. COFFEE 4-1-1857
SMOOT, THOMAS TO MARY F. HAMMER 12-8-1863 (12-10-1863)
SNELLING, ALLEN TO HANNAH RAINS 9-23-1865 (COL)
SNELLING, LAURA TO WESTLY SMARTT
SNEPS?, MARY C. TO J. T. GARTH
SNIDER, E. R. TO JANE FRAZER 11-30-1865
SNIPES, B. F. TO SOUSAN C. C. WATKINS 11-15-1855
SNIPES, CYNTHIA C. TO C. K. SPIDEL
SNIPES, JAMES A. TO THURSA A. NEBLETT 11-25-1865
SNIPS, SARAH E. TO SIDNY F. EDWARDS
SNOWDEN, ALIDA W. TO J. HENRY RODES
SOAPE, JANE TO WM. GOODWIN
SOAPE?, JANE TO WM. GOODWIN
SOLOMON, ELIZABETH TO SAMUEL RODGERS
SOLOMON, NANCY JANE TO WM. CLARK
SORELL, GEORGE C. TO MARY ANN SEALS 3-21-1853 (3-22-1853)
SOWEL, MATILDA TO ELIJAH SPURLOCK
SPANGLER, LEVINA TO H. H. WOODS
SPARKMAN, LOUANA TO SAMUEL CHRISTAN
SPARKMAN, M. B. TO NANCY ANN MILLER 12-15-1852 (12-19-1852)
SPARKMAN, NELSON TO MARGARET CAMPBELL 11-12-1852
SPIDEL, C. K. TO CYNTHIA C. SNIPES 12-18-1856 (12-25-1856)
SPRING?, CAROLINE TO JOHN W. LOCKHERT
SPURLOCK, EDMOND C. TO SARAH BLANTON 9-30-1858
SPURLOCK, ELIJAH TO MATILDA SOWEL 9-14-1858 (9-16-1858)
SPURLOCK, JAMES M. TO JOSEPHINE A. SMARTT 11-12-1856
SPURLOCK, MELISSA TO THOMAS ROBERTS
SPURLOCK, REBECCA L. TO JAMES SULLINS
STANDLY, AGNES C. TO JOSEPH BALES?
STANLEY, A. T. TO PARALEE T. KELLEY 8-9-1860 (8-10-1860)
STANLEY, MARY ANN TO J. H. MCNEELEY
STANLY, JAMES C. TO NANCY DUNHAM 2-27-1858
STARKEY, MISSABYLE TO JAMES? M. BASSHAM
STARNES, C. C. TO ----- 8-29-1857
STEBBINS, JULIETTE C. TO J. G. KIRKPATRICK

STEMBRIDGE, HENRY R. TO ELIZABETH VANHOOZER 3-7-1855
STEMBRIDGE, JOHN TO JANE CANTRELL 1-3-1854
STEPHENS, SOUSAN TO ABRAHAM CARTER
STEPP, JOHN A. TO MANERVA MCGEE 3-28-1859 (3-31-1859)
STEPP, WILLIAM C. TO NANCY J. MCGEE 9-6-1857
STEWART, CATHERINE TO GEORGE D. HOPKINS
STEWART, CHARLES W. TO ELIZABETH C. CLIFT 9-4-1865
STEWART, FRANCES A. TO BENJAMINE COLLINS
STEWART, MARY TO WM. NEWLY
STEWART, SARAH TO MARSHALL N. SMITH
STEWART, TELFORD TO SARAH R. MCWHORTER 11-5-1852
STILES, A. M. TO NANCY G. THOMAS 1-5-1864 (1-6-1864)
STILES, JOHN TO LITITIA ROWEN 9-3-1860 (9-4-1860)
STILES, MARY TO ANDERSON RANDOLPH
STILES, SAMUEL TO LAURA M. FOWLER 5-7-1863
STOCKSTILL, LERINA TO WM. FREEMAN
STOGSTILL, LOUISA TO W. J. ESCUE
STONE, H. J. TO S. P. PENNIBAKER
STONE, HENRY D. TO MARY E. WARE 10-13-1855 (10-17-1855)
STONER, DELPHA TO DAVID RIDE?
STONER, VINEY TO JOHN E. BISHOP
STOTTS, MANERVA TO JOHN BARROTT
STOVALL, J. C. TO M. D. STUBLEFIELD 10-25-1859 (10-26-1859)
STRAUBE, FRANCES C. TO WM. S. SAPP
STROUD, B. F. TO SOUSAN E. JONES 12-1-1858
STROUD, CARY TO RACHEL PEAY 11-18-1866 (SB 1865) (12-3-1865) (COL)
STROUD, COOPER TO ANICA RAMSEY 10-2-1865
STROUD, D. A. TO LOUZETTER MATHEWS 9-24-1863 (9-27-1863)
STROUD, GEORGE TO ANGELINA G. NELSON 4-10-1860
STROUD, M. L. TO HARRIETT POWELL 12-4-1855 (12-6-1855)
STROUD, MANERVA N. TO ROBERT C. HENDERSON
STROUD, REZI TO NANCY WALLING 5-9-1856
STROUD, SARAH TO ALEXANDER POWELL
STUBBLEFIELD, CATHARINE TO JAMES N. CLENDENON
STUBBLEFIELD, LEONEDUS TO NANCY HOODENPYLE 10-5-1858
STUBBLEFIELD, MARY S. TO J.? W. JOHNSON
STUBBLEFIELD, W. H. TO M. A. COLVILLE 10-24-1863
STUBLEFIELD, M. D. TO J. C. STOVALL
STUBLEFIELD, NARCISSA V. TO THOMAS J. HOUSTON
STUBLEFIELD, SARAH TO CLABERRY FULTS
STYLES, E. J. TO ROMULUS MACON
STYLES, JAMES TO JANE MCDOUGAL 9-10-1858 (9-12-1858)
STYLES, JULIA M. TO WILEY C. RANDOLPH
STYLES, MARTHA TO DANIEL FULTS
STYLES, ROBERT TO ELIZABETH MORROW 10-10-1852
SULLENS, JOHN TO ALCEY E. GREEN 9-6-1859
SULLINS, JAMES TO REBECCA L. SPURLOCK 8-18-1860
SULLIVAN, MARTHA B. TO J. G. MOHLER
SUMMERS, ELI J. TO MALINDA J. PRICE 11-1-1853 (11-7-1853)
SUMMERS, M. C. TO C. A. HOLLAND 7-6-1863
SUTTLE, EMELINE TO JACOB BLACKBOURN
SWAN, W. T. TO S. C. BRIXEY 11-30-1865
SWANEY, MARTHA TO JOSEPH HANEY
SWANN, W. J. TO L. C. BONNER 11-11-1865 (11-12-1865)
SWANN?, MARTHA E. TO CALVIN L. BRICKEY
SWANN?, MARY E. TO JOSEPH T. WALKUP
SWEET, OTHENIEL TO MATILDA LOWRY 4-19-1858
SWINDLE, JAMES TO TURY? GRIBBLE 4-17-1862 (WITH 1861 ENTRIES)
SWINDLE, WM. TO REBECCA DOBKINS 3-27-1854
TALLEY, CALEB TO MARY WRIGHT 9-7-1863

TALLEY, JAMES H. TO MARTHA ANN POWELL 11-15-1865 (11-16-1865)
TALLEY, MARTHA TO WILLIAM HENNESSEE
TALLY, JOSEPH C. TO CLEMENTINE PEPPER 9-21-1865
TALLY, MARGARET TO THOMAS J. SMITH
TANNER, ELIZA TO WILLIAM BELL
TATE, DICEY M. TO R. H. KELTON
TATE, ELIZABETH TO ISHAM DYKES
TATE, HARRIET TO ASAHEL WEBB
TATE, JAMES D. TO MARY JANE MCGREGOR 1-13-1858
TATE, LAURA TO ISAAC ANDERSON
TATE, MALINDA TO JAMES COPPINGER
TATE, MARY G. TO D. C. BALLUE
TATE, SARAH TO GEORGE JACKSON
TAYLOR, COLUMBIA N. TO W. C. NICHOLS
TAYLOR, ELLEN V. TO J. N. LANCE
TAYLOR, FRANCES A. TO J. C. MCDANIEL
TAYLOR, FRANKEY TO JARLEY CAGLE
TAYLOR, H. J. H. J. TO ELIZABETH J. MACON 7-17-1865
TAYLOR, JOSEPH W. TO S. M. SMALLMAN 9-24-1861
TAYLOR, MALISA A. TO JAMES T. WINDHAM
TAYLOR, MARTHA TO JOHN D. CAGLE
TAYLOR, MARY TO WM. RAMSEY
TAYLOR, MATILDA TO JOHN GRIM TEMPLE
TAYLOR, NANCY A. TO EZEKIEL MORGAN
TAYLOR, WILLIAM E. TO ROSANAH REEDER 9-2-1859 (9-4-1859)
TEMPLE, JOHN GRIM TO MATILDA TAYLOR 8-8-1853
TEMPLETON, JAMES M. TO MARY ANN MCGEE 10-18-1862 (10-19-1862)
TEMPLETON, REBECCA TO JACKSON QUICK
TEMPLETON, SARAH TO HENRY WANNER
TEMPLETON, WM. TO ANNE QUICK 4-27-1856
TEPLES, JOHN TO CATHARINE MARTIN 5-17-1858
THAXTON, H. J. TO AMERICA BONNER 10-4-1853 (10-5-1853)
THAXTON, JOHN B. TO ELIZA JANE HENNESSEE 8-2-1858 (8-3-1858)
THAXTON, MARTHA AN TO GREEK BRAWLY
THAXTON, MARY TO WM. J. HUMBLE
THAXTON, NANCY M. TO JOHN A. SISSOM
THAXTON, SAML. TO GILLY KING 9-18-1865 (COL)
THAXTON, SARAH E. TO T. J. BELL
THAXTON, WM. M. TO CLERICA BONNER 12-6-1854
THOMAS, ELVIRA TO JACOB KEEZEY
THOMAS, HAMP TO WILLIAM T. SMARTT
THOMAS, NANCY G. TO A. M. STILES
THOMASON, J. W. TO AMANDAH ALLEN 7-9-1854
THOMPSON, DELPHA TO ISAAC BROWN
THOMPSON, THOS. J. TO RHODA H. SMITH 11-29-1860 (12-22-1860)
THORP, A. D. TO L. A. MARTIN 7-26-1863
THURMON, O. M. TO LOUCINDA JONES 10-22-1857 (10-31-1857)
TIPTON, LEVINA TO G. W. MCDANIEL
TIPTON, MARTHA JANE TO JOSEPH BYBEE
TITSWORTH, JOHN P. TO ELIZABETH BYARS 7-25-1853 (7-25-1853)
TITSWORTH, MARTHA TO WILLIAM A. POTTER
TITSWORTH, RICHARD M. TO POLLY WAMACK 11-14-1859 (5?-15-1859)
TITTWORTH, THOMAS M. TO MARTHA W. BYARS 12-23-1852
TODD, DAVID TO SAROAH ELAM 10-29-1853 (10-31-1853)
TODD, NANCY TO T. C. ROBERSON
TOSH, JOHN TO PERMELIA M. BROOKS 6-30-1856 (7-2-1856)
TOSH?, TRACEK? TO MARY ANN MCDARNILD 8-16-1854
TOUHY, JOHN TO MELVINA OWENS 9-27-1855 (9-29-1855)
TOWLES, ELIZA TO C. C. MURPHEY
TOWLES, J. S. TO SARAH S. WOOD 4-16-1862

TRAMEL, DANIEL TO DEDAMEY VANHOOZER 5-14-1858 (5-16-1858)
TRAMELLE?, WM. TO MARGARET E. E. BROWN 8-19-1856 (8-24-1856)
TRAMMEL, ELIABETH TO SAMPSON VANHOOZER
TRAVIS, D. M. TO H. A. JONES 4-25-1863
TRAVIS, D. M. TO JANE C. WILKERSON 1-10-1854 (1-17-1854)
TRAVIS, DANIEL TO MARGARET VANHOOZER 8-1-1853 (8-8-1853)
TRAVIS, F. W. TO MARTHA N. WILSON 6-28-1862 (6-29-1862)
TRAVIS, MARIA TO LARRY SMARTT
TROTT, H. AMANDAH TO STEPHEN BANKS
TUCKER, GRANVILLE TO MALINDA J. CAMPBELL 11-11-1853
TUITUR?, J. J. TO SARAAH BISHOP 1-30-1854 (2-2-1854)
TURNER, ANDREW J. TO KITTEY ANN AIKINSON 3-3-1853
TURNER, CAROLINE TO JEFFERSON SAVAGE
TURNER, JEFFERSON TO MARGARET OVERTURFF 11-28-1859 (11-29-1859)
TURNER, MARGARETT TO WILLIAM B. CHRISTIAN
TURNEY, ISAAC TO MALINDA FINGER 1-2-1862
UNDERWOOD, THOMAS J. TO MATILDA HARGEST 11-27-1865
UNDERWOOD, W. R. TO MARTHA WORTHY 12-22-1856
UPCHURCH, JOHN TO ELIZABETH WEBB 2-17-1857 (2-19-1857)
UPCHURCH, MARTHA TO WM. C. ROWLAND
UPCHURCH, MARY TO JAMES M. LAWS?
USSEREY, ELIZABETH TO PHILIP BLACKBURN
USSERY, LESA TO ISRAEL LUTHER
USSERY, SARAH TO T. J. COUCH
VADAMS, JAMES C. TO LOTTY CROSLAND 10-5-1852 (10-6-1852)
VAN, JAMES TO MARY DAVIS 8-10-1859 (8-11-1859)
VANHOOSER, BARBARRY TO JASPER GWINN
VANHOOSER, EULYSSES TO HANNAH NEWBY 9-4-1861 (9-5-1861)
VANHOOSER, ISAAC J. TO JANE CANTRELL 1-30-1860
VANHOOSER, REBECCA TO JOHN BARKER
VANHOOSER, SARAH TO JAMES HUDSON
VANHOOSER, W. J. TO LOUIZA JONES 2-13-1865
VANHOOZER, DEDAMEY TO DANIEL TRAMEL
VANHOOZER, ELIZABETH TO HENRY R. STEMBRIDGE
VANHOOZER, MARGARET TO DANIEL TRAVIS
VANHOOZER, NANCY TO WM. FREEMAN
VANHOOZER, SAMPSON TO ELIZABETH TRAMMEL 11-27-1855
VANHOOZER, SOUSAN J. TO G. G. L. ESCUE
VANNERSON, J. HENRY TO M. J. SMITH 12-24-1861
VAUGHN, A. G. TO EDMOND HOLFERD
VAUGHN, GEORGE W. TO CHARITY E. HOLLAND 1-28-1862
VICKERS, ELLEN TO JAMES L. MARTIN
VICKERS, M. J. TO B. F. JONES
WADE, C. A. TO R. J. WILSON 11-10-1860 (11-11-1860)
WADE, P. M. TO MILDRED SETLER 12-13-1853
WAGANER, JOSEPH TO NANCY RUTLEDGE 9-29-1858 (10-29-1858)
WAGONER, MATHIAS TO ELIZABETH BROWN 8-6-1857
WALDON, E. S. TO LOUISA E. ELAM 3-3-1858
WALKER, ALEXANDER TO JULINA HASSA? 11-13-1852 (11-14-1852)
WALKER, ALEXANDER TO MARY ALLEN 8-15-1863
WALKER, JUDA F. TO WILLIAM GIVINS
WALKER, W. W. TO MARGARETT COLLIER 9-27-1861
WALKER, WILLIAM TO LUCY E. WILSON 8-22-1864 (8-23-1864)
WALKUP, JOSEPH T. TO MARY E. SWANN? 1-27-1858
WALLACE, NANCY TO CYRUS BONNER
WALLACE, W. H. TO LETTY ANN PRATER 10-15-1863
WALLACE, WM. D. TO MARY E. MCLENELL? 9-28-1857
WALLING, ALFRED TO ELIZABETH PATTERSON 8-23-1865 (COL)
WALLING, J. D. TO HARRIET L. GREEN 11-20-1854 (11-21-1854)
WALLING, JESSEE TO BELL WINTON 10-6-1863 (10-7-1863)

```
WALLING, NANCY TO REZI STROUD
WAMACK, AMERICA M. TO FRANCIS M. CANTREL
WAMACK, B. R. TO MARY WEBB 11-13-1858 (11-15?-1858)
WAMACK, CAROLINE TO WILLIAM DAVIS
WAMACK, ELIZABETH TO ISAAC CLARK
WAMACK, JOHN M. TO NANCY GOODSON 3-27-1855 (3-29-1855)
WAMACK, JOHN TO NANCY FULTON 11-25-1852
WAMACK, MARY TO L. D. KENT
WAMACK, NANCY P. TO J. W. COUCH
WAMACK, POLLY TO RICHARD M. TITSWORTH
WAMACK, SURRILDA TO THOMAS WAMACK
WAMACK, THOMAS TO SURRILDA WAMACK 6-22-1852
WAMACK, WILLIS TO SARAH DAVIS 7-29-1853 (7-31-1853)
WANNER, HENRY S. TO SARAH TEMPLETON 1-22-1855
WARD, E. J. TO W. H. ----GS
WARD, JAMES R. TO CAROLINE NUNNELEY 10-14-1858
WARE, ALLEN TO ESTHER L.? REED 10-18-1856 (10-19-1856)
WARE, ANN TO W. P. HARRIS
WARE, MARY ANN TO LAUSON MARTIN
WARE, MARY E. TO HENRY D. STONE
WARE, THURSDAY A. TO WM. NEBLETT
WARE, WILIE TO LETTY ARGO 9-30-1852
WARE, WILLIAM TO ELIZA WILLIS 10-6-1860 (10-7-1860)
WARREN, ELIZABETH TO J. H. PHILIPS
WARREN, JAMES TO MARY GREEN 1-7-1856
WATERHOUSE, JONATHAN TO REBECCA REACE 9-16-1865 (COL)
WATERS, E. C. TO WM. H. NORTH
WATH, ELIZABETH TO SIDNEY CUMMINS
WATKINS, SOUSAN C. C. TO B. F. SNIPES
WATLEY, NANCY TO STEPHEN CRUSE
WATLEY, W. T. TO N. S. HAYNES 11-24-1859
WATSON, LOUISA E. TO PULASKI DELAFAYETT WEBB
WATTERMAN?, E. P. TO H. S. LANE
WEATHERFORD, ALEX TO SELINA CLARK 6-17-1860
WEBB, ASAHEL TO HARRIET TATE 10-31-1856 (11-2-1856)
WEBB, CAROLINE TO W. C. BESS
WEBB, CROCKETT TO HANNAH WEBB 1-15-1861
WEBB, CYMANTHIA TO JAMES S. GRIBLE
WEBB, DIDAMA TO W. J. PENNINGTON
WEBB, DIDEMA TO J. STURT SMITH
WEBB, DIDEMY? TO G. W. MEDLEY
WEBB, ELIAS TO NANCY MCPHERUN 12-13-1853
WEBB, ELIZABETH TO GEORGE DENTON
WEBB, ELIZABETH TO J. S. WILLIAMS
WEBB, ELIZABETH TO JAMES H. FAULKNER
WEBB, ELIZABETH TO JOHN UPCHURCH
WEBB, ESTHER S. TO ADAM RHEA
WEBB, GEO. W. TO JULY D. GIBBS 10-22-1863 (10-23-1863)
WEBB, GEO. W. TO MARYANN HANEY 12-16-1862
WEBB, HANNAH TO CROCKETT WEBB
WEBB, JAMES SR. TO CATHARINE WINDS 3-23-1863 (3-24-1863)
WEBB, JOHN TO RACHEL ALLISON 10-27-1856
WEBB, JOSEPH TO ELIZABETH JONES 8-29-1857
WEBB, LEVY TO MARY SMITH 2-11-1858
WEBB, MARY TO B. R. WAMACK
WEBB, NANCY TO CALEB PENNINGTON
WEBB, P. G. TO MARY J. YOUNG 12-18-1858 (12-22-1858)
WEBB, PULASKI DELAFAYETT TO LOUISA E. WATSON 8-8-1856 (8-10-1856)
WEBB, R. D. TO RUTHA DENTON 11-3-1860 (11-4-1860)
WEBB, REBECCA TO SOLAMON ELLIS
```

```
WEBB, SARAH TO BENJAMIN F. HICKS
WEBB, SARAH TO ISAIAH RODGERS
WEBB, THOS. TO LOUISA WYMS 9-22-1852
WEBSTER, WILEY TO JENNIE MEEKER 10-29-1865
WEST, M. C. TO ELIZABETH AKERS 7-4-1859
WEST, MARY E. TO JESSEE BARRETT
WEST, NANCY TO ROBERT BROWN
WHEELER, A. D. TO MARY A. NORTHCUTT 10-26-1865
WHEELER, E. J. TO SAML. COMER
WHEELER, JAMES A. TO MARY E. FINGER 9-3-1857
WHEELER, SARAH TO G. A. M. NEWLY
WHEELER, SARAH TO SAML. RAMSEY
WHEELING, PARSETA TO J. W. BRATCHER
WHERLEY, RHODA TO WILLIAM SELLERS
WHITE, MAHULDAH TO WILLIAM HAYNES
WHITE, MARTHA JANE TO MORGAN D. HAMPTON
WHITE, MARY J. TO R. J. FUSTON
WHITE, MARY JANE TO R. J. FOUSTON
WHITE, SARAH TO JOHN H. ROYAL
WHITE, WM. H. TO MARY J. POPE 10-25-1865
WHITLOCK, JAMES K. TO DAVID A. JACOBS 3-20-1857
WHITLOCK, JAMES TO SARAH FREEMAN 7-25-1857
WHITLOCK, KATHARINE TO JOHN MULLINS
WHITLOCK, KULS? TO RODA PITTS 12-2-1857
WHITLOCK, SOUSAN TO JOHN HEART
WHITMAN, E. D. TO POLLY CLAY  10-1-1860 (10-2-1860)
WHITMAN, EDWARD? TO SELA? BOST 9-7-1854
WHITMAN, JEREMIAH TO ELIZABETH GREEN 6-12-1856
WILCHER, JULIA F. TO WALTER B. LUVARD
WILEY, JOHN TO NANCY A. MEDLEY 5-21-1862
WILHOIT, LEVY E. TO LUENTIN T. LOYNE 8-27-1852 (8-26?-1852)
WILKERSON, CLARASY TO HARVEY H. KEELE
WILKERSON, DOCTOR TO TELITHA ELLIS 4-9-1863
WILKERSON, J. M. TO MARY MARTIN 8-9-1861 (8-10-1861)
WILKERSON, JANE C. TO D. M. TRAVIS
WILKERSON, MARTHA C. TO JAMES ROWLAND
WILKERSON, SAML. TO SARAH BRATCHER 12-11-1862
WILKERSON, SARAH TO JAMES P. GREGORY
WILLIAMS, EDWARD TO MARY F. CUNNINGHAM 4-25-1861 (4-30-1861)
WILLIAMS, J. S. TO ELIZABETH WEBB 11-11-1864
WILLIAMS, MARGARET TO C. A. MCDANIEL
WILLIAMS, MAXEY TO JASPER BAIN
WILLIAMS, MYRA TO JESSEE SAVAGE
WILLIAMS, PARALEE TO MICHAEL BORIN
WILLIAMS, W. J. TO MARYE? ELLIS 4-9-1859 (4-10-1859)
WILLIAMSON, N. R. TO N. A. HERNDON 12-3-1853
WILLIS, ELIZA TO WILLIAM WARE
WILLIS, WILLIAM C. TO JUDAH MITCHELL 2-2-1857 (2-3-1857)
WILSON, AVEY TO GEORGE W. READER
WILSON, C. C. TO EUDORA M. SELLERS 12-31-1856 (1-1-1857)
WILSON, D. M. TO MARTHA YORK 8-7-1862
WILSON, ELIZABETH TO JAMES R. WILSON
WILSON, ELIZABETH TO THOMAS RAINS
WILSON, ESTHER TO THOMAS MARSHALL
WILSON, FANNY B. TO JOSEPH L. JONES
WILSON, H. H. TO NANCY J. AKERS 6-26-1854 (7-6-1854)
WILSON, JAMES R. TO ELIZABETH WILSON 11-10-1857
WILSON, JAMES TO ELIZABETH MASE 9-21-1865
WILSON, JAMES TO ROSANAH REEDER 10-8-1859
WILSON, JESSEE TO BETSEY MASTON 1-23-1862
```

WILSON, LUCY E. TO WILLIAM WALKER
WILSON, M. J. TO JOHN W. GILLEY
WILSON, MARGARET TO THOMAS K. KENNEDEY
WILSON, MARTHA N. TO F. W. TRAVIS
WILSON, MARTHA TO LUTHER DUNLAP
WILSON, MARY TO HUGH F. HOPKINS
WILSON, MARY TO JAMES MCDANIEL
WILSON, NANCY JANE TO GEORGE M. SAVAGE
WILSON, R. J. TO C. A. WADE
WILSON, SQUIRE TO PATSEY DAVIS 11-24-1865 (COL)
WINDHAM, JAMES T. TO MALISA A. TAYLOR 5-14-1860
WINDHAM, N. J. TO JOSEPH K. MACON
WINDS, CATHARINE TO JAMES WEBB SR.
WINTON, BELL TO JESSEE WALLING
WINTON, GILBERT TO NANCY BONNER 6-26-1858
WINTON, JOHN TO NANCY BONNER 10-24-1857
WISEMAN, AUDLEY TO MALVINA GILLENTINE 7-1-1863
WISEMAN, ELIZABETH TO MARTIN MCGEE
WITT, MINERVA J. TO ISAAC V. LYNN
WITTEY, HANNAH E. TO M. B. ROBERSON
WITTEY, J. B. TO M. E. FAUSETT 12-28-1857
WITTEY, JAMES J. TO SARAH F. DOSS 1-8-1862
WOMACK, A. E. TO MALINDA DAVIS 10-6-1865
WOMACK, FELIX G. TO SARAH E. COPE 4-16-1864 (4-19-1864)
WOMACK, JAS. J. TO TENNIE G. AMONETT 3-20-1862
WOMACK, MELVINA TO RUFUS SIMPSON
WOOD, F. A. E. TO H. J. CAMPBELL
WOOD, OBEDIAH TO VIRGINIA E. ORRICK 11-8-1864
WOOD, SARAH S. TO J. S. TOWLES
WOOD, VIOLA H. TO J. C. ALEXANDER
WOOD, WILLIAM J. TO ANNA ARMSTRONG 12-20-1865 (12-21-1865)
WOODLEE, A. J. TO LOUVISA BARNES 10-13-1863 (10-20-1863)
WOODLEE, D. H. TO CAROLINE MURFREE 12-3-1860 (12-4-1860)
WOODLEE, ELIJAH TO MIRA MAYSEY 12-15-1853
WOODLEY, JOHN L. TO MARY MCKNIGHT 1-19-1859 (1-20-1859)
WOODLOE, HARRISSON TO DOVEY CATHCART 7-31-1854
WOODS, H. H. TO LEVINA SPANGLER 3-25-1860
WOODS, R. M. TO ANN HENNESSEE 12-31-1856 (1-1-1857)
WOODS, ROSANER B. TO ROBERT H. RHEA
WOODS, THOS. J. TO REBECCA FOSTER 1-18-1854
WOODWARD, MIRA A. TO M. V. GRIBBLE
WOODWARDS, MACOM H. TO HANNAH M. GRIBLE 9-14-1858 (9-16-1858)
WOOLDRIDGE, MARY TO AARON HUGHES
WOOLF, NEWSOM TO MARY DARNELL 1-5-1861 (1-6-1861)
WOOTON, ANN TO BENJAMINE MCGEHEE
WOOTON, BENJAMINE TO BETTY WOOTON 9-25-1865
WOOTON, BETTY TO BENJAMINE WOOTON
WOOTON, JAMES TO MARTHA BRYANT 9-25-1865 (COL)
WOOTON, MARTHA J. TO A. B. DAVIS?
WOOTON, WESLEY TO BETTY MCGEHEE 9-25-1865 (COL)
WOOTTON, DAVID TO M. J. GUYNN 12-5-1853 (12-6-1853)
WORD, WM. C. TO CLEMENTINE CLARKE 12-28-1853 (1-25-1853?)
WORLEY, MARY ANN TO DAVID RICHARDSON
WORTHY, MARTHA TO W. R. UNDERWOOD
WRIGHT, E. J. TO LUCINDA MCDANIEL 10-21-1852
WRIGHT, MARY TO CALEB TALLEY
WRIGHT, NANCY TO HIRAM CUNNINGHAM
WYMAN?, JAMES TO MARY MASON 1-1-1855
WYMS, LOUISA TO THOS. WEBB
WYNNES, RUTHA A. TO JAMES A. DURHAM

YAGAR, EDWARD TO SALLIE ANN SMITH 7-25-1853 (7-26-1853)
YORK, FRANCIS TO PAIRLEE ANN FOUSTON 11-2-1853
YORK, HENRY TO JANE HENEGAR 10-19-1854
YORK, MARTHA TO D. M. WILSON
YORK, ORLANDER J. TO MIRTHA? E. SMITH 12-8-1858 (12-9-1858)
YORK, PERLINA TO JOHN C. HENEGAR
YORK, SILAS R. TO H. J. DOUGLASS 4-10-1856 (4-11-1856)
YORK, WM. L. TO SARAH HILLER 1-8-1853 (1-11-1853)
YORK, WM. M. TO ELIZABETH HUTCHISON 3-23-1853 (3-30-1853)
YOUNG, MARY J. TO P. G. WEBB
YOUNG, WM. C. TO MARY ELWIN 11-17-1853
YOUNGBLOOD, M. L. TO JOHN C. DAVIS
YOUNGBLOOD, W. T. TO NANCY E. FARLEY 10-15-1863